On Faith, Works, Eternity, and the Creatures We Are

READING AUGUSTINE

Series Editor:

Miles Hollingworth

Reading Augustine offers personal and close readings of St. Augustine of Hippo from leading philosophers and religious scholars. Its aim is to make clear Augustine's importance to contemporary thought and to present Augustine not only or primarily as a pre-eminent Christian thinker but as a philosophical, spiritual, literary, and intellectual icon of the West.

On Faith, Works, Eternity, and the Creatures We Are

André Barbera

BLOOMSBURY ACADEMIC
NEW YORK • LONDON • OXFORD • NEW DELHI • SYDNEY

BLOOMSBURY ACADEMIC
Bloomsbury Publishing Inc
1385 Broadway, New York, NY 10018, USA
50 Bedford Square, London, WC1B 3DP, UK

BLOOMSBURY, Bloomsbury Academic and the Diana logo are trademarks of
Bloomsbury Publishing Plc

First published in the United States of America 2020

Bloomsbury Publishing Inc does not have any control over, or responsibility for,
any third-party websites referred to or in this book. All internet addresses given
in this book were correct at the time of going to press. The author and publisher
regret any inconvenience caused if addresses have changed or sites have ceased
to exist, but can accept no responsibility for any such changes.

A catalog record for this book is available from the Library of Congress.

ISBN: HB: 978-1-5013-5607-0
         PB: 978-1-5013-5606-3
         ePDF: 978-0-5676-8977-1
         ePub: 978-0-5676-8979-5

Series: Reading Augustine

Typeset by Integra Software Services Pvt. Ltd.
Printed and bound in the United States of America

To find out more about our authors and books visit www.bloomsbury.com
and sign up for our newsletters.

Just as he accepted slavery, so he accepted time.
(Augustine, Enarrationes 74.5)

CONTENTS

PREFACE

A few years ago I had the good fortune to receive a sabbatical leave from St. John's College. I devoted that year to reading about faith and works, a subject that has long held my interest. I am troubled by the relationship of works to faith. This book is a result of studies initiated during that year. I did not set out to write a book about St. Augustine, and in a sense I have not. As my work advanced, however, I began to realize how influential his writings had been on my thinking, especially regarding the intersection of the eternal with the temporal.

Many people—colleagues, students, friends, Vincentians—have shaped my thinking about faith and works. I deeply appreciate their comments, advice, criticism, and concern. I mention here only a few who have contributed directly to this book: my colleague Jon Tuck who got me to read more Kierkegaard; Paul Dry of Paul Dry Books who suggested that I express my thoughts in direct, personal terms; Miles Hollingworth, the general editor of the Reading Augustine series, who devised the series to begin with and who has advised, supported, and encouraged my efforts; my colleague Ron Haflidson who informed me of the series and who has offered useful suggestions regarding the text; and Mary Barbera, the love of my life. She abides.

1

Introduction to the Problems

I wonder about faith: faith in God, faith in reason, faith in country, faith in a lover. What is the relationship of faith to works? What does the person of faith do, or not do, and how does he do it? We are creatures of faith. We believe, we trust, and we attempt to act in accord with our belief and trust. We also doubt, betray, and live inconsistent and disintegrated lives. These failings belong to the creatures of faith, to all of us. We, the faithful, are also the unfaithful, but we are not the faithless.

My interest in the relationship of faith to works is hardly unique. To the contrary, this relationship is of universal concern, a matter of interest for all persons of faith, for each and every one of us: for the lover, for the patriot, for the secularist. Here, however, I am principally concerned with faith in the God of Abraham, and especially with faith in this God as understood by Christians, the God who gave his only begotten son. What does the Christian do? How does he act faithfully, and what good, if any, is faithful action?

As I began to investigate the relationship between faith and works, to study the interconnecting mechanism of faithful action, it became apparent to me that despite my faith in faithfulness—we are all creatures of faith—I did not and do not know who are the faithful. One might say, I do not even know what faith is, although I have learned that faith and faithfulness are not identical. I have also learned that the demands of faith cannot be met because they are inherently contradictory. Thus I find myself at a point where I charge each and every one of us with infidelity. Matters, however, are worse than mere infidelity. My answer to the question "Can one *know* that one believes?" is an emphatic "*No.*"

From this perplexity has come my inquiry, an inquiry into a struggle. The inquiry itself is a struggle, one in which I have illustrious predecessors, notably Søren Kierkegaard, but I include also the Apostle Paul and St. Augustine of Hippo. Augustine especially has shaped this study with his comments on time.

Here at the beginning I am confronted with problems. A problem is something put forward, a task, a fence, an excuse. In one regard, it seems as though I present the problems to myself, I throw them before me: What is faith? Who believes? How does the person of faith act? But if I am correct in my assertion that we all are creatures of faith, then in another regard the problems present themselves. Our part consists in attending to the problems, and that is what I attempt to do with this study.

* * *

Theology, including accounts of atheism, must be the most excellent of human studies owing to the majesty of the object of inquiry, God. The question of God weighs on man more heavily and presses him more urgently than any other question. For us the significance of the word "God" is as great as it is uncertain. Commonly one encounters the claim that God is always and everywhere a question. Even more common is the assertion that God is the answer. Perhaps the indefinite and definite articles should be exchanged in these assertions. God is always and everywhere the question. God is an answer. As an answer, God intensifies and deepens the very questions that lead to God. Faith is not the end (cessation) of questioning but rather the true beginning. Despite the ever-present depth of its inquiry, however, theology also must be the most pretentious, impertinent, and foolish of human studies, to the extent that it attempts to reason methodically about the unknowable. If there is a divine judge who metes out eternal reward and damnation, then surely he imposes a unique and most horrific punishment on those who misrepresent him. Like Job's counsellors, theologians are in need of intercessory prayer.

We are all, deep in our hearts, theologians, but only a few have the temerity and impertinence to write out their theological speculations. This work is intended to be theological. It may justly be called psychological, skeptical, disingenuously open-minded, and irreverent. At times this inquiry may appear to be engaged in anthropology, history, and ethics. These connections are incidental. My primary intent is to inquire about faith in general, more particularly about faith and works, and especially about the actions of the Christian. On the one hand, the inquiry is not explicitly confessional, in that it does not cite and hold to a foundational creed, although the influence of my Roman Catholic upbringing, training, and practice will be evident. On the other hand, the inquiry is manifestly Judeo-Christian, especially Christian, and it makes regular recourse to the Bible as a source of wisdom.

The Bible: Old and New Testaments, Tanakh and Christian Scripture. It is one thing to assert that these writings are a source of wisdom. This puts them on a par with the writings of Shakespeare. It is perhaps claiming something more, but not much more, to say that the Bible is a unique source of wisdom. One can go a little further and claim that the Bible is divinely inspired. These assertions do not amount to much more than saying that the Bible is a book revered over the ages by many for its teaching and for many other reasons. It is a foundation for Western thinking.

The Bible is the word of God. "That word is spoken eternally, and by it all things are uttered eternally" (Augustine, *Confessions* XI.vii.9). On the face of it, this looks like a genuine advance in that the word of God presumably could not be in truth contradicted. The word of God is the truth. But if this is so, then we must inquire into what is meant by "word of God," leaving aside for the time being concerns about truth and God. I find attractive Karl Barth's claim in *The Epistle to the Romans* that the Bible is the word of man from which the word of God attempts to break forth. The reader of the Bible, the recipient, must allow the word of God to break forth, but this allowance is no easy task, no mere passivity. Indeed, the allowance is a mighty, perhaps superhuman, struggle. One must engage with the Bible, the word of man, in order to make room for the breakthrough. One must fight with the text.

As vivid and appealing as the notions of engagement and struggle may be, we must ask ourselves how to distinguish between such an encounter with the word of man and the self-serving selection of apt expressions and phrases to support a thesis or opinion. The theologian, having formulated a proposition, then goes searching for support—a confirming parable, story, or account in the Bible. (Everyone does this.) Having found the appropriate phrase or expression, he brings it forward as evidence, divine testimony to support the ideas of men. Thus we are faced with the problem of deciding which is which. (1) Humble engagement with the word of man in the hope and with the faith that the truth that is alleged to have been revealed in the Bible will in fact be revealed to us. (2) *Ex post facto* cherry-picking. On the face of things, (1) and (2) look alike.

No one, no human being, comprehends the word of God. No one grasps firmly what has been said. The word of God, by its very transcendence, is beyond us. It is too big, too deep, too far away. In fact, the word of God is not too much of any magnitude, finite or infinite, for mankind. It is not simply of a different order of magnitude. No, the word of God is qualitatively different from the word of man, and thus no intensification of man's comprehension will be up to the task. We rational beings understand infinite expansion, although we certainly do not imagine it. But infinite expansion of our understanding in no way meets up with the word of God.

On the assumption that the Bible is the word of man through which the word of God is attempting to break forth, I conclude that our encounter with the Bible begins with the word of man but does not originate with mankind. Were the encounter to originate with mankind, then this investigation would be radically different from the one presented here. It would be anthropological or psychological, but not theological.

Finally, I must make two more assertions very clear. First, attempts to tame the Bible must be resisted. The history of preaching and biblical exegesis consists largely of exactly this: an attempt to tame, to shackle and domesticate the teachings of the Bible, to make them more palatable and less exceptional, less outrageous. I assume that my outrage at biblical claims, and especially at the words of Jesus, is a sure sign of their interest to me. I may find many things interesting, but I have *an interest* in these remarks. My outrage points further to the second assertion. Second, the Bible's teaching comes from without. It is revealed to us. It is not merely the words of men inspired by the Holy Spirit, although it may consist exactly of those inspired words.

In this study, I have relied on the writings of many authors other than the Bible, many of whom are Jewish or Christian theologians. Although these authors are truly magisterial and their thinking capacious, the resultant work here is narrow. Different sources would have produced different results, although perhaps equally narrow. Absent here are authors from the East, mystical or meditative writings, and consideration of religious practices other than those of Judaism and Christianity. No attempt is made to inquire into feeling. My work might also be charged with being graceless in at least two senses.

This inquiry into faith and works presents an argument of sorts, consisting of interconnected parts. These parts all fit together, at least in the mind of the author, but they are spread out sequentially in chapters. The chapters do not lend themselves entirely to a linear unfolding, although much of the argument follows from the postulate at the end of this introduction. The work here is not definitional. It is, rather, work on faith. I *use* definitions, especially the one in the Letter to the Hebrews. These are starting points.

The relationship of works or deeds to faith has generated much comment over the centuries, some of it contentious. Disputes have arisen among various Christian denominations as to how works issue forth from faith, and particularly regarding the role, if any, that works play in the salvation of the individual Christian. It is not my intention to address directly these disputes, and at no place has the argument below been crafted to resolve points of disagreement. More generally, let me note that this inquiry into faith represents solely the thinking of the author, who does not speak for any religious sect or denomination.

* * *

It is commonly remarked that all questions and problems of theology reduce themselves ultimately to questions about time. Such has been my experience as I have endeavored to study and to think about faith and works. Accordingly, I shall find it necessary, especially given the postulate at the end of this introduction, to make a few remarks about time, although they are mostly negative or equivocal. I propose to speak about eternity, and the inquiry into faith unfolds from the tension, perhaps one should say contradiction, between eternity and time. The terms of discourse shape the argument, and ordinary language may be an inadequate medium for thinking about time. I affirm, nonetheless, the postulate in order to investigate the temporal condition of faith, a condition that turns out to be paradoxical. Furthermore, I acknowledge boldness on my part in speaking about time as if everyone was in agreement as to what time is. Is it one? Is it at all? I beg the reader's indulgence here (and in many other places) as I attempt to initiate the inquiry.

Most important for the consideration of the eternal is an investigation of succession and consequence. Does time form the basis for all such considerations, or can we understand relation and logical entailment independently of time? Is there meaning to the claim that all was made through the creator ("all things are uttered eternally"), and without the creator was not made at all that which was made? Specifically, did God create time? Many theologians, including those who have produced profound meditations on time, such as Augustine, answer affirmatively. And yet I shall consider the suffering aspect of time, especially as it relates to faith. In this regard, time will appear to have more in common with sin than it has with God's good creation. We often speak of time as if it were one, although our dealings with time are varied. In one case time seems to be original with us, and in another case it seems to be external, an imposition that we suffer.

I shall speak of God, the creator, and wonder if the terms "being" or "object of faith" can in any way do justice to what is intended. If one accepts the postulate, then at least in one respect the creator is not a being, and certainly the creator does not exist. Following a line of theological speculation, I suggest that the creator is that which is supremely.

God, of course, is not the only object of faith. Along with the variety of objects come various kinds of belief and trust, and these in turn condition our lives variously. Our faith may be placed in a lover, in gold, in Dulcinea. Each of these objects is a god for the person of faith. Although the sources drawn from here are preponderantly theological and Christian, I believe that many of my claims can be extended, with some modification, to pertain to these other objects of faith.

God himself will receive a variety of designations, such as person-God, omni-God, and eternal action. With a liberal interpretation of God, or gods, and a corresponding liberal interpretation of adoration, there seems to be no such thing as complete or perfect atheism. Most people worship several gods and so, conversely, monotheism is practically impossible. We, the faithful, live contradictory lives.

Prudence, or something like it, haunts these pages as well as my efforts to navigate through some of the turbulence of contradiction, although that virtue seems to be antithetical to the zeal for truth normally associated with faith. If faith is a virtue, even if it is a divinely inspired virtue, it is a worldly one like prudence that is subject to time and shaped by circumstance. The goal may be transcendent, unwavering, eternal, but the pursuit is muddled and filled with what looks from the outside to be compromise. Human beings are to varying degrees faithful, unfaithful, prudent, and imprudent. A good conscience weighs in the balance.

Central to the argument set forth in this study is the understanding of faith as a quest for knowledge or wisdom, knowing, and the struggle that ensues from pursuit of this understanding. In developing this notion, I rely on arguments from Augustine, St. Thomas Aquinas, John Calvin, and others. These authors combine to argue persuasively that an end of faith, perhaps *the* end of faith, is knowledge.

"Faith seeking understanding" stakes the claim. The notion, perhaps a mistranslation of Isaiah 7:9, is promulgated by Augustine and taken up by St. Anselm of Canterbury. But Jesus provides the key link in his parenthetical observation about eternal life: it is knowledge. "And this is eternal life, that they know thee the only true God, and Jesus Christ whom thou hast sent" (Jn 17:3). This interpretation is confirmed by Paul, Aquinas, and Calvin. Faith is the pursuit of eternal life.

There are various kinds of knowledge. Some knowledge is factual, worldly, and contingent. Some is logical and necessary. Augustine distinguishes between wisdom and knowledge. The former concerns eternal things and the latter concerns temporal ones. Crucial to the argument set forth is the role that time plays in the knowing. I assume that the knowledge of eternal life, at least in its eternality, is independent of time. This is a contentious claim. The argument here accepts the assumption in order to explore the tension and conflict that necessarily ensue from pursuing the eternal. If the emphasis is placed on life rather than on eternality, and if life is to be taken in more than a metaphorical sense, then time re-enters into the considerations. The Incarnation, an affront to the understanding, epitomizes the confusion to which eternal life points.

The person of faith seeks a level of knowing beyond his comprehension. He seeks the beatific vision. Equally incomprehensible is the union of the eternal with the temporal, the Incarnation of Jesus Christ. A common union, a fitting together, comes about whenever a temporal being understands and contemplates the necessary, but the Incarnation is a union of a different kind. It is unique. Can Jesus Christ be known in any way other than as the man Jesus of Nazareth? But knowledge of Jesus Christ the Son of God is exactly part of the reward, achievement, or eternal condition of temporal faithfulness, according to Jesus. I shall investigate the impossibility of attaining such knowledge in our lifetime. Given this state of affairs, the pursuit of eternal life (faith) is at best a struggle and it may be futile.

The person of faith, or aspirant to faith, is also doubly in the dark. He seeks not only knowledge about the object of faith but also about his own faithfulness. Our own trustworthiness is always at stake. According to Augustine and Aquinas, to believe is to think with assent, and we must know what constitutes assent. We must also investigate that which is to be believed. Is it a person or a proposition? If it is a person, then how do we believe that person? Do we trust what he says to be the truth, or do we simply trust that the person cares for us? Do we trust Jesus when he says "I am the truth"? If what is to be believed or assented to is a proposition or statement, then we must inquire into the meaning of the proposition irrespective of its veracity.

The inherent contradiction between the mode of faith and the objective of faith leads to anxiety. Contradiction and anxiety can be found in all forms of faith, not just in the pursuit of eternal life. This is so because we human beings are creatures of faith and likewise are sufferers of time. In this state the person of faith, a sinner, must act. Necessarily he performs works and obeys, and I inquire into the evidential nature of these works and obedience. They may be signs of faith, but they are not eternal life.

The connection of faith to works by means of anxiety appears to be a psychological solution to my motivating question, and such an understanding is possible. The introduction of sin, however, refashions the solution whereby we leave the realm of psychology to enter that of religion. One might be anxious for a variety of reasons and, in turn, there may be a variety of anxieties. Some of these might be identified with historical periods, but the anxiety of faith is not historical, or perhaps more properly it is all-historical, since it is inextricable from faith itself.

Luther, relying on Paul, asserts that no one loves the Lord with all his heart, soul, and might. Thus no one keeps the law, not even the First Commandment, and we worship many gods. For this investigation I accept the all-or-nothing theology of Paul, and thus part ways with the more pragmatic and accommodating thinking of many theologians. A consequence of my position is that we all become idolaters, and we know it.

The person of faith who is self-aware, who knows himself as a sinner, becomes particularly anxious, and for him anxiety manifests itself in works. Even without the acknowledgment of sin, this person acts and obeys. This may seem to be a psychological response, not a theological one. But along with my liberal interpretation of God or gods comes an equally liberal interpretation of theology. The person of faith who betrays does not sin against God but "sins" against god. Thus the faithful-unfaithful one is also anxious before god, although this person does not describe the condition as sinful.

One might wish for works and obedience to be evidence of faithfulness. We cannot be certain. The works *are* evidence of anxiety. Are these works also a sign for the believer? Can the faithful person give himself a sign? Some signs are reliable and some are not. The problem with the First Commandment is that it is directed to the interior of man. Keeping the commandment requires a special kind of self-knowledge, a kind that is normally not needed by the thief or the adulterer.

Faith is worldly. Central to all matters of faith, from the point of view of the believer, is existence, i.e., the passing of time, waiting, and suffering. Faith can be ridiculed as waiting in pursuit. We wait for that which we cannot receive temporally. Unlike the postulate at the end of this introduction, *we* are bound by time. "I still do not know what time is … [but] I know myself to be conditioned by time" (*Confessions* XI.xxv.32). How close is the essence of man to his existence? Is "essence of man" a meaningful expression? This condition, our existence, in itself would not present a problem for us if we had no understanding of the eternal, if we were completely illogical, or if we believed that temporality formed the foundation for all succession, both contingent and necessary. The working hypothesis here is quite the opposite. Man seeks consistency and integrity in a world of change, and would like to conduct himself in a way that accords with his beliefs. This desire coupled with belief leads to a code of conduct. A lover, Don Quixote, a Christian: each acts in certain ways, dutifully. Lurking in these actions is complacency, the notion of progress in the quest of faith. But the construction of a life of faith, properly understood, consists of never-ending struggle. The rock of faith upon which one stands is submerged in the sea and covered with slime and seaweed. The result for us is increased anxiety.

The person of faith seeks to live an integrated and righteous life. He seeks to be worthy of the happiness that he hopes to receive. In short, he desires to be right, whether standing before a personal god or confronting the impersonal way things are. In either case, the believer's self-respect is at stake. The world, others, may approve or disapprove, finding the individual to be right or wrong. The person of faith, however, also seeks to appear right or justified before himself, a quest that cannot be completed in this life. In fact, the quest cannot even be begun with certainty. (My assertions here should not be interpreted to mean that the righteousness and justification sought by the faithful may be achieved after this life, to mean that the reward may be received in the next life, the life that follows this one.) In the personal relationship, be it with another person or with a person-god, the particularity of the individual is reflected into the object of faith. The believer holds the object in esteem and assumes its integrity. Thus, in the case of the Son of God become man, the person of faith is utterly befuddled. Not only has eternity been fused with time, but also the universal has taken on particularity. Truth has been embodied. That which is supremely has been confined and defined.

Knowledge is the goal of faith. Will all receive the same reward? Are all worthy? Does each person have the same capacity to be rewarded? In this world those who know seem to be as varied as things known. And although there is great uniformity of belief among us, we differ on important particulars: this person, that country, Jesus Christ. Can we all also be one in Christ?

Calvin argues that justification is the reward for true faith in Christ, by which he means absolution of sin and removal of guilt. Augustine claims to aspire to a condition of rest. Given the characterization of the individual presented here, intermittently faithful, fighting, living a life of contradiction, both absolution and rest seem desirable. But rest is a temporal condition. We are unable to cling to the eternal, no matter how frequently we touch it. Is there eternal rest? This question is clearly related to the one about eternal life. What might the life of truth be like?

The person of faith, the disciple, seeks to surround himself with like-minded people, people in the same condition as he is in. Some, like Pope Francis, argue that faith is public, not private; it is communal and relational. Certainly, one needs a sign, some sort of revelation in order to believe. Perhaps one can seek a sign in communion. Since faith is a constant struggle, one might look to fellowship as a temporary solution to a temporary problem, temporal balm for a temporal wound. Such support, however, would need to be continuous and life-long to be effective, and even in this case the effectiveness would be confined to this world. The alternative is to persevere on one's own, lonely, fully in the grip of original sin. For sin manifests itself as estrangement. The corrupt nature of man is evident in the abandoned sinner. Religion, to the extent that it refers to anything other than the relationship between the Creator and creation, provides the fellowship of aliens to aliens.

Time and sin test religious faith at every turn. Without time and sin, faith is meaningless. Except for some revelatory signs, the sinner lives almost entirely in the dark, although he has the companionship of other sinners. Can he know where he stands? Can he test things not known for certain? Both Moses and Jesus warn against testing the LORD, and yet the very thrust of faith is to know, to *see* the results. We want to make ourselves into faithful servants, and we desire certainty that our efforts are not in vain. What else is religious fasting other than an attempt to express faithfulness and obedience, to demonstrate to ourselves and perhaps to others and to God that we are trustworthy? Can we derive a measure of confidence from our past actions that we deem faithful, perhaps from a single faithful act? We are also familiar with our sinful past, our duplicitous present, and we can reliably predict our inconstant future. Along with the Apostle Paul, our best desire and our certain knowledge are in conflict. Again, we confuse time and eternity.

The act of faith, the obedience, is evidence. It is a sign, but the interpretation of signs is a tricky business. The same event (sign) can appear miraculous to one person and magical to another.

Faith is "assurance of things hoped for" (Heb. 11:1). If there is comfort or consolation to be found by the believer, other than in companionship, then it must be in the things hoped for: knowledge, wisdom, rightness, rest. The latter has been deemed temporal, and yet the Christian prayer for the dead seems to combine, or perhaps confuse, the eternal with the temporal: "Eternal rest grant unto them, O Lord, and let perpetual light shine upon them." We receive encouragement in the Bible from the likes of Jesus and Paul to take solace, if not in our faith per se, then in the object of our faith, the heavenly Father. We are encouraged to trust in God's faithfulness.

The person of faith goes beyond hoping for good things in this life and the next or other life. The believer prays. How prayer works remains a mystery. In order to understand the power of prayer, one would first need to understand the workings of the world absent of prayer. Specifically, one would need to know the eternal plan for a temporal unfolding. A miracle can be defined, as can efficacious prayer, but identifying a miracle as distinct from magic requires belief.

The Incarnation is a name for a particular mixing of the temporal and the eternal, the unique mixture. Consideration of the Incarnation leads to thinking about the Crucifixion and the Resurrection. Being able to say who or what died on the cross in turn leads to an interpretation of the Resurrection story. I shall provide a mere sketch of four possible answers to this question.

The first and only likely answer is that Jesus of Nazareth, a man judged to be a criminal and blasphemer, died on the cross. The next two answers proceed from the corollary of the postulate, i.e., from the Incarnation. The Son of God, the creator become creature, was embodied in the man Jesus of Nazareth. These are the answers of orthodox Christian theology. Jesus Christ comprised two natures but one person, one hypostasis or substance. These possibilities return us to a central problem of this inquiry, the intersection or blending of the temporal with the eternal. One nature of Jesus, that of man, is to live and to die. The other "nature" of Jesus, that of God, is neither to live nor to die. Our fourth answer is that in every respect God died on the cross.

The first and fourth answers lead to specific kinds of atheism. Christianity is a hoax, or Christianity truly entails the death of God. With each of the four answers, the person of faith is also re-imagined, from accepting comrade to envious compatriot, from glorified individual to general principle. My consideration of the Crucifixion also leads to an inquiry about Jesus' self-knowledge. I ask with particular reference to a most troubling encounter, related by Matthew and Mark, between Jesus and the Canaanite woman.

The only plausible answer (a man died) and the implausible (God died) both lead to a rejection of Jesus Christ, the Son of God. The blood of the cross leaves its historical mark in either case. Godless religion, which has always existed, takes on Christian specificity. There are religious atheists, praying, conducting rituals, holding meetings on Sundays. Even the Christian answers can lead, less directly and perhaps insidiously, to the same rejection of Jesus as the Son of God. We come to understand the Son of God as a son. The face of Christ becomes the face of man. Jesus Christ becomes truly our brother in every respect. He is no more or less the child of God than is each of us.

* * *

POSTULATE: GOD IS NOT BOUND BY TIME

I use various designations for God: person-God, omni-God, and eternal actor. This God is often thought to be the creator of all that there is, including time. Thus concludes Augustine: "There was therefore no time when you had not made something, because you made time itself" (*Confessions* XI.xiv.17). As complex as time may be, even if it is both interior and exterior, I shall usually speak as if time were one. Time may extend indefinitely, that is infinitely into the past, or infinitely into the future. On the contrary, one often sees the assertion that there is something like a temporal beginning to time and a temporal end to time, although such assertions, at least superficially, appear to be nonsense. The postulate accommodates all these possibilities. It does not accommodate the understanding of time as sinful, an imposition brought on by the sinner and suffered by him. If this too is time, then time is not one. The postulate begs only that God be eternal, timeless. God does not coexist with time. This creator could make time such that it always was and always will be. Thus the beginning of time, "in the beginning," is not in the past, nor is the end of time in the future.

2

Is Time?

Much of my study could be interpreted as a commentary on time, and yet I do not investigate time per se. There is no talking or thinking about time that is entirely satisfactory, but this parlous state may be owing equally to the seeming multiplicity of the subject itself. Is time one? We speak as if it is, and yet our thoughts about and experiences of time indicate a multiplicity of times.

The primary reason for offering any comments whatsoever on the subject of time is to consider logical entailment as an encounter with non-temporal action, an eternal act. In order to do so, I must say something about succession, and I must consider if succession is meaningful without time. Is temporality the underpinning for all succession? Must we believe in time in order to understand and derive logical entailment, or can we conceivably reverse the order? I propose to do just that, even if the proposal is merely an article of faith. I assert that we have an adequate understanding of logical succession, what I am calling "eternal action," independent of our notions of time and temporality. Such an assertion, a belief, is necessary to pursue the implications of the postulate: God, *the* actor—Augustine's Word—acts eternally. His creating is a-temporal, although we the creatures "see" time everywhere that we look in his creation.

* * *

We commonly speak about time as if it were a thing, like the Statue of Liberty, a stone, matter, or beauty. We tell time. We keep time. We waste time, and suddenly we are out of time. Speaking thus, especially along the lines of "losing time" or "losing track of time," betrays the mind of a sufferer, one for whom time is a foreign problem, an alien. One frequently loses track of time while playing, for in play we surmount time. But when the play ends, we re-enter time. We become aware again of our temporality and comment on its suspension during play. In play, as players, we authorize, but having exited the game or play we return to an inauthentic life of observation and suffering.

Most of us also balk at the notion of time's thing-hood, and when asked what time is, we wind up concurring with Augustine who claims that he knows what time is provided that no one asks him to explain it (*Confessions* XI.xiv.17). Are things in time, or not in time? Aristotle, elaborating on his assertion that neither motion nor rest are in time, writes that those things that cannot be, such as a side of a square commensurate with the diagonal, cannot be in time (*Physics* 221b.22–4), nor can the opposites be in time, such as the incommensurability of the same side and diagonal, which always (ἀεί) is (*Physics* 222a.4). (By "always," does Aristotle mean for all time, or is the scope even larger than temporality?) Aristotle's reliance on a mathematical relationship, the incommensurability of the side and the diagonal, provides a key as to how we might understand the eternal as logical entailment. Incommensurability *follows* logically from a group of geometric definitions, common notions, and postulates, specifically those of Euclidean geometry. But this incommensurability does not temporally come *after* the postulates, nor do the postulates come *before* the relationship of the diagonal to the side. The postulates create the relationship.

Augustine tells a joke about the non-temporal notion of before. "What was God doing before he made heaven and earth? ... He was preparing hells for people who inquire into profundities" (*Confessions* XI.xii.14). Augustine rejects the answer because it does not address the profound importance of the question, specifically the meaning of "before" (*antequam*). For Augustine, before does not have temporal significance; it does not refer to time. Thus the Word who was with God, and who is God, and through whom all things are made (Jn 1:1-3) "is said in the simultaneity of eternity. Otherwise time and change would already exist, and there would not be true eternity (*aeternitas*) and true immortality" (*Confessions* XI.vii.9). Augustine further analyzes the beginning of the Gospel of John, and in doing so points to the very tension between time and eternity that generates my study of anxious faith. He divides the gospel claims into two groups according to wisdom and knowledge. The statements about the Word and creation belong to wisdom, and hence are eternal. Those concerning the light shining in the darkness and the man sent to bear witness to the light belong to knowledge, which Augustine classifies as temporal (*De trinitate* XIII.1.2, 343). Thus, for Augustine, eternity means "outside of time," truly timeless. In the joke, the "before" must therefore indicate another kind of relation, one that is non-temporal. I call this "eternal action" divine creation.

One can read the great thinkers on time—Aristotle, Augustine, and many more—in search of nouns, a definitional name for time. Time is *x*. Here I shall merely present what I call the ordinary or common understanding of space and time, an understanding that serves us moderately well. Space is conceived as the ultimate container in which material things including our bodies are located. The extent of the container is left unspecified. Along with this container there is time, a running clock that pertains to the container and its contents but is separate. The clock is not material. The things in the container exist; they subsist in time. They are measured in a way by the clock. Space and time, commonly called dimensions, are independent of one another. Furthermore, they are independent of our perceiving or conceiving of them. In short, both space and time are absolute. Things are located in space and subsist in time.

Immanuel Kant proposes various conceptions of time, one of which is absolute time. But he prefers to describe time as our intuition of order or succession of appearances (*Critique of Pure Reason* B49–50). For us to perceive simultaneity or succession, time must be present a priori in us (*Critique of Pure Reason* B46). The effect of my postulate is to deny this understanding, at least as it might pertain to the creator.

Since the seventeenth century, natural scientists have developed a mathematical representation of the common understanding of time and space. Conventionally, space is represented by three mathematical dimensions or variables, x, y, z. These variables are represented in a Cartesian system of coordinates, with axes that are interchangeable with one another. A fourth dimension, variable t for time, may not be interchanged with the spatial axes.

In the early twentieth century, Albert Einstein and Hermann Minkowski demonstrated the inadequacy of this representation.

They showed that when considering two coordinate systems in uniform rectilinear motion with respect to the other, the spatial coordinate of one system may have time as part of its expression in the other system. And the temporal designation of one system when translated into the other system always has at least one spatial coordinate as part of its expression. Thus the ordinary conception of time and space allows for interpenetration. Ultimately, the distinction between t and any one of the other three variables is eliminated.

The Einstein-Minkowski model assumes what has been called the ordinary or common understanding of space and time and shows the interrelation between the dimensions. The problem is that the common understanding, at least in its mathematical rendition, is incorrect. Even clock time is not exactly clock time.

There are, of course, many other ways to think about time than according to a clock. Martin Heidegger, in *Being and Time*, insists on the foundation of temporality for all understanding of being by *Dasein*—his term for man existing. Time is an outgrowth of this foundation, and all thinking about time by us, by human beings, must begin by rooting itself in this foundation. Any attempt to go beyond or around this foundation amounts to overreaching on the part of the human being. I presume that Heidegger would reject my postulate and thoughts about succession. They would constitute exactly what he prohibits: an attempt to speak about the eternal, as if one could circumvent one's temporality.

A consideration of time, of course, need not be restricted to the quantitative and Western treatments mentioned here. One cannot help but note that, in all such considerations, the terms of discourse shape the meaning, or perhaps one should say, the terms of discourse are the meaning.

Equally pertinent to and problematic for this discussion of time are words that express being. The verb *to exist* connotes a sense of time, specifically *being in time*. Thus, to claim that the Statue of Liberty exists makes sense, as does the claim that it existed in 1940. I assume that it also makes sense in a way to claim that "The Statue of Liberty existed in 1840." In the latter case, the meaning of the sentence is clear and one judges the assertion to be false. I would like to restrict use of the verb *to exist* to those cases where time is clearly intended, and now consider some cases in which *to exist* is inappropriate.

Aristotle claimed that the incommensurability of the diagonal of a square with its side "always is." *Exists* is the wrong word in this context (the incommensurability ... exists) because it introduces time where it does not belong. Adding "always" (ἀεί) may in fact confuse the meaning if by always is meant everlasting. In that sense, time has been reintroduced into the expression and extended infinitely.

This inquiry might gain some precision if it were conducted and expressed in one of the Romance languages that has two verbs for the English *to be*: the French *être* and the German *zu sein*. Spanish, for example, has *ser* and *estar* (Latin *stare*). The latter word has a temporal quality to its meaning, indicating being at a time and in a place. The former is more like a copula. The following is a useful, even paradigmatic comparison: *estar borracho* and *ser borracho*. The former means "to be drunk," whereas the latter means "to be a drunk." Were this study to be conducted in Spanish, not only would *existir* (to exist) be avoided in those cases where the intent was to express the timeless, but also *estar*.

It is from this vantage point that I ask, awkwardly, the question that serves as the title for this chapter. Heidegger may have preferred the question "Is there time?" But the "there" has a connotation of location, and accordingly of temporality, which of course would have been Heidegger's point to begin with. Thus I stick with my formulation and answer "yes" tentatively. Better yet, I shall translate the question and answer into Spanish: *Es tiempo? Sí.* My diffidence, however, arises from the following concerns.

From the affirmative answer one may not conclude that time exists. If time existed, there would be multiple times, one enclosing another. This is Augustine's reasoning. There may very well be infinitely many times, with each greater time subsuming the lesser. All together they would constitute a fullness of time.

"What is time?" may be the wrong question. This study may be laboring under a compulsion to define that which it seeks to deny in a special case, to categorize that which, although it is often assumed to be one, has many aspects. The postulate of the previous chapter has led to an inquiry about time. I may require or beg of the reader that God not be bound by time, but then I should attempt to say something about the alleged freedom. I now arrive at the central purpose for making these remarks about time: to consider consequence or entailment and the eternal.

Can we understand logical entailment or consequence without a background or underpinning of time? Do we have access to the meaning of the postulate or, more severely, does the postulate have any meaning? If temporality is the foundation for succession, a precondition for understanding even necessary succession such as logical entailment, then the answer is "no." One then is forced to say that time is the condition or foundation of succession, although we may have done no more than give a common name, temporality, to another common notion, succession. But if time can be removed from logical entailment, even if only *ex post facto*, then an insight into the eternal may be possible. But which is the precondition, time or succession? The method of investigation employed here, discursive thinking and writing, is prejudicial to the inquiry by seeking to understand consequence without time, to extirpate time from succession. The postulate demands not the removal of time but rather an acknowledgment of our addition of time.

Let me begin by considering examples of succession. In all cases it is assumed what has been assumed all along, that one reads from left to right and that one reads from line to line down the page rather than continuously on a single line. The indulgence of the reader is requested here in the presentation of collections of discrete elements, three in each case, while assuming a unique encounter with or apprehension of each element. To identify the relationship between the elements as first, second, and so forth would prejudice the endeavor. Furthermore, I use the term "succession" merely to distinguish among the elements.

Consider the following three successions, each on a line, with commas indicating the succession of items in each series.

╟, ╢, ╥
c, d, e
3, 4, 5

In the first example, the order of symbols or figures seems to be entirely arbitrary. One would be hard pressed to argue why another order such as ╥, ╟, ╢ would be preferable or prior to the original. The second example displays a portion of the alphabet in conventional but also arbitrary order. The argument in favor of the original in lieu of *d, e, c* rests on convention. The third example gives three counting or natural numbers in their "natural" order: *4* is *the* successor to *3*, and *5* is *the* successor to *4*. Other arrangements are possible, but these would violate the normal order of succession. The norm is to arrange the numbers according to the successor operation, specifically the number that follows *n* traditionally and operationally is *n+1*.

Now consider two more minimal sequences, each comprising two elements or parts. In fact, I am considering consequence, but by "to follow with" (*consequi*) I do not mean "to come after temporally." First, I assume the definitions, common notions, and postulates of Euclidean geometry, either those that appear in Euclid's *Elements* or modern substitutes and expansions. Note that the geometric version of the Pythagorean Theorem, Propositions I.47 and I.48 in the *Elements*, follows from this assumption. Most notable is the dependence of these propositions on Euclid's Fifth Postulate, the parallel postulate, or on a systemic equivalent.

Second, with the same assumptions regarding Euclidean geometry, Aristotle's claim about the incommensurability of the side and diagonal of a square follows. A demonstration of the consequence does not appear in Euclid's *Elements*, but the consequence can be demonstrated in strictly Euclidean and geometric fashion.

There are five examples: three series and two examples of consequences or logical entailment. Now one is in a position to ask if time underpins all succession. Let the three figures of the first series be spread out so that one encounters one figure ⊩, and then after a while another ⫤, and after another period of time the third ⟂. As three figures in a series, one encounters them successively in time. There is no reason for this arrangement and accordingly one does not know the succession except that one does know the will of the author. The other two series are different in that, at least conventionally, one knows the successors. For example, given *a, b, c, d, e*, one knows by convention what follows. Is time or temporality a part of this knowledge? One certainly cannot claim a natural or inherent order here, i.e., an arrangement in which human beings are not a part.

The counting numbers present a more complex case. We understand in that realm the notion of successor. Proofs of mathematical induction rely on this understanding. Is this an order which, although known by the human mind, is independent of that mind? Richard Dedekind denies the possibility and asserts that numbers are free creations of the human mind, independent of our spatial and temporal intuitions ("Nature and Meaning of Numbers" 31). Thus, for Dedekind, although we remain within the realm of human thinking, we are free from dependence upon time.

Heidegger would disagree, not only with Dedekind regarding numbers, but also with Aristotle regarding the timelessness of the incommensurability of the side and diagonal of a square. For him all succession, even logical entailment that I assign to the realm of the eternal, is rooted in temporality (*Being and Time* H18–19, H227). This is so, he claims, because it is we (*Dasein*) temporal beings who understand and make sense out of such succession. Existing supports all succession.

If we are inextricably existing beings—and in a sense we certainly are—then we must remove time from arbitrary succession. The appearance of ♮ and ♯ I take to be entirely arbitrary, by which I mean that reversing them, ♯ and ♮, is of no or only arbitrary significance. We must say the same about d and e, because we acknowledge the convention of the sequence. We know the sequence in the same way that we know a historical fact, as contingent. But with Heidegger's position, the symbols or letters are arbitrary only because I can reverse them, but my reversal is not truly original and creative. Just as I encountered the symbols temporally, so do I temporally invert them. This line of thinking would effectively reject my postulate about God and time. It would also reject Augustine's understanding of creation.

Now I consider privation, moving beyond series to consequence. One understands that Euclid's Fifth Postulate is a necessary precondition for the Pythagorean Theorem. One can imagine historically an undeveloped version of Euclidean geometry that contains the Fifth Postulate but in which the Pythagorean Theorem has yet to be discovered. The reverse of this historical arrangement is a temporal order according to which many persons come to know aspects of geometry. Some may first learn the Theorem without much if any justification for its validity. Others may learn the Theorem in its spatial or geometric application, the validity of which is learned through experience, such as in carpentry and gardening. Subsequently, some may study the definitions, common notions, and postulates of Euclidean geometry, as well as the unstated conditions such as the force of the *reductio ad absurdum* argument, and only then move on to the necessity of the Fifth Postulate for the Theorem.

Thus constitutes the history of learning, but such is not my primary or positive concern here. Indeed, much of learning from experience consists of encountering the effect first in time, and only subsequently determining the cause. I seek to remove or deprive time from the relationship between the Fifth Postulate and the Theorem. But, by removing time, I have decided the question in advance. Time was there between the Postulate and the Theorem, but in wishing to demonstrate pure cause and effect I had to obscure the temporal foundation by pretending to remove it.

Must time be removed from logical consequence? Must one believe in existence first and foremost? Rather than removing time, what if one uncovers the timeless? What if the eternal reveals itself to us in logical entailment and, as I have claimed, what if we acknowledge that we are the ones who introduce time? What if time is not the basis of succession, but rather succession the basis of time? It is not as though we are no longer temporally bound. "I know myself to be conditioned by time" (*Confessions* XI.xxv.32). But at some level we understand consequence and effect. Indeed, we know that consequence flows in one direction. We do not understand that the Fifth Postulate follows from the Pythagorean Theorem.

Let me connect fancifully Aristotle's assertion about the incommensurability of the side and diagonal of the square with my claims about a-temporal consequence. Let there be a creative being with superior geometric and logical knowledge. Let the being choose Euclidean geometry, i.e., a geometry with the Fifth Postulate or its equivalent, and choose it because it is good. This being thus knows that with its choice comes the incommensurability of the side and diagonal of the equiangular, equilateral quadrilateral, the square. Perhaps such a choice is good because definite incommensurability is a good thing. Consider the Lobachevskian alternative, in which "squares" of varying sizes are not similar. Accordingly, among the infinitely many kinds of "squares," there are infinitely many instances where the side-diagonal ratio is commensurable, and infinitely many instances where it is incommensurable. Evil? Let us call the Euclidean case universal incommensurability, which of course follows from the choice of the Fifth Postulate. To say that it follows means that it is known, a logical and geometric consequence, which is known by our creative being.

I return to the postulate of the previous chapter: God is not bound by time. These negative and equivocal comments about time should not be misconstrued as an attempt to deduce the postulate from prior and more primitive notions. Certainly, I have not done that. Quite to the contrary, I have attempted to show the need for the claim to be a postulate. But more is attempted here, to show that there is something truly interesting about the postulate, that it contains a claim that one can approach, that one can attempt to understand. If I have succeeded in showing the possibility of logical entailment independent of time, then the appeal of the postulate should be evident. For then we may be in a position to consider Augustine's God, and mine, an actor outside of time. According to Augustine, this God creates time.

I propose that God creates time analogously to the way in which the Euclidean definitions, common notions, and postulates create the Pythagorean Theorem as well as the incommensurability of the side and diagonal of a square. These are actions of a sort, independent of time. There is an actor of sorts, although about the actor, its being, little if anything can be said. One points to the effects. (Most of theology consists of pointing to the effects.) Indeed, in the case of the eternal actor, I am reluctant to refer to it as a being. I am equally reluctant to assert without equivocation that God creates time, for, as I shall propose, time as perceived by us can be regarded as sinful. I shall not consider God as the origination of sin, and thus time must be understood from multiple perspectives.

Consider again the title of this chapter and note that the previous answer to the question posed there, "yes," may have been hasty. To the question "Is Time?" an answer better suited to this study is "yes and no."

With my postulate and these remarks about succession and entailment I mean to posit a being independent of time. Things, at least some things, come first. I fully acknowledge a kind of boldness, perhaps even to the point of recklessness, on my part in asserting priority for some being. Even cursory general remarks about being would lead me far astray from my intended goal to study the relationship between faith and works. My belief that some things, God, come first has already been implied in the postulate: God is not bound by time. In that statement I presuppose that "God" refers to that which is. The reference is sloppy and analogic—it is a belief—but not meaningless.

Briefly, I consider other beings. The definitions, postulates, and common notions of Euclidean geometry may be taken as beings or a being. In such manner, they are the cause. Propositions I.47 and

I.48, the geometric Pythagorean Theorem, are the effect. Implied in my postulate is that this relation, logical entailment, is taken as a foundation. Accordingly, succession and then time would follow from being, but they would not temporally come after. They would originate in the being. The Pythagorean Theorem originates in the Fifth Postulate. I extend this argument by applying it to the eternal actor, to God. Another expression of this "being" is supreme being, that which is supremely.

As necessary as it may be for us to name God, all the names are inadequate, analogical, and in a sense blasphemous. Among these names, "supreme being" may be as damaging as any. This expression does not refer to a being that is superior to other beings, the being supreme among beings. Such an expression might be fit for Zeus.

I have adopted a circumlocution that is hardly original with me. God is that which is supremely. How God may reveal himself as the origin of time is another matter. But if we adopt a notion similar to Augustine's that God is Being and only God is Being, then time in one of its manifestations may be a consequence.

Language, of course, shapes the argument. In my attempt to indicate the eternal, I have used the expression "timeless." The term, like "atheist" in another context and "nonbeing" in yet another context, grants a kind of priority to that which is being denied. Our language betrays a privative aspect that one might like to avoid in referring to the eternal. I also have claimed that logical consequence "flows" in one direction. The expression has a metaphorical quality, as if one thought along with Marcus Aurelius of time as a river. And in my attempt to free us from the notion of privation in considering time, I claim that we do not "remove" time from the relationship of logical entailment. Rather, we "uncover" the relationship.

With respect to the word "eternal," note that *aeternus* is variously translated as "eternal," "everlasting," and "always." Augustine's remarks (in some of his writings) indicate that he means what here has been called eternal, i.e., timeless, rather than the notion of lasting forever, time unending.

With Aristotle's remarks regarding incommensurability, we find the word ἀεί, which is commonly translated as "always" or "forever." I understand Aristotle to mean what Augustine indicates with *aeternus*, timeless. Like "exist," "forever" conveys time never ending, going on and on. "Always," too, is usually understood in this sense, although there may be a way of thinking of all-ways as encompassing and superseding time (the fullness of time).

I anticipate a similar problem of translation or interpretation as we proceed to the main argument of my study of faith. In the expression "eternal life" (αἰώνιος ζωή) I have understood eternal in the manner of Aristotle and Augustine. One might have translated αἰώνιος as "everlasting," an interpretation rejected here.

By starting with be-ing, the alpha and omega of gerunds, I have postulated some things first. At least, I assert Being (God) first. On the face of it, "all is in flux" says nothing. Some thing stands under: substance. Change not only implies permanence but depends entirely upon it.

I return now to the matter of making a positive statement about time, although it may amount to no more than bad poetry. Let us reject the neat categories of time suggested by Kant, in lieu of which we consider a condition called time that is both the *sine qua non* for human (not eternal) experience of order or succession, and a suffering. One might call it "fallen-ness" in the biblical sense. Thus time would have both an inner and an outer aspect. Time would subsist both as part of the constitution of rational, sentient beings and as that which afflicts those beings. One might even regard time as sin.

Although is it very difficult, perhaps impossible, to speak with assurance about time, it is real. The reality of time, however, does not imply that time exists. There are seemingly innumerable interpretations of time, a few of which have been mentioned above, and the experience of time is varied even for a single human being. I do not know if such variety is owing to circumstance and thought, or if it results from a multiplicity of independent and separate things, each confusedly called "time." Even if there is but one time, real time lends itself to an understanding of its aspects. Or perhaps, more properly speaking, we, according to our discerning nature and ability, express our disintegrated being in our attempts to talk about time. "You are my eternal Father, but I am scattered in times whose order I do not understand" (*Confessions* XI.xxix.39). Thus there may be at least an echo of sin in these attempts.

By sin I mean disorder between the Creator and the created individuals who say "I." The disorder is one of culpability on the part of the individual. The individual who says "I" wills the disorder. The individual responsibly brings about the disorder. But the disorder does not have a temporal origination in this sense. The disorder is fundamentally temporal in being, but not in occurrence. It is not an event. Indeed, the disorder is in a way a qualification for all events, a necessary underpinning. I understand original sin, or more precisely its manifestation, to be not only loneliness but also the relationship of time to eternity, a relationship that is confusing.

If time is real, and if not-time, eternity, also is real, then they seem to exclude one another. Similarly, freedom and necessity cancel out one another. But what if the eternal intersects with the temporal? What if we, in our temporal being, understand eternal relationships, logical entailments? Even more to the point, what if God became man?

By faith, we bring logical entailment into the world of experience. We apply necessity to existence. In so doing, we give evidence that we are redeemable, that we, rational, sentient, temporal beings, are capable of being right, of being justified. As such beings, of course, we never know our own righteousness. I do know that all who proclaim with an air of righteousness do so hypocritically. Even when they are right—and who can tell?—they act unrighteously. But I speak here not of the certainty of redemption or salvation but merely of its possibility. In short, we have access to Jesus Christ. The impress of the creator is upon the creature. That we avail ourselves of this access is by no means assured. That Jesus of Nazareth is the Christ is by no means assured. We do not know that we have been redeemed. We are told so. It is revealed to us. Some people confess that they believe what they have been told.

Thus can our sinful nature be truly evil? "The LORD saw that the wickedness of man was great in the earth, and that every imagination of the thoughts of his heart was only evil continually" (Gen. 6:5). I rephrase the question: is having a heart that is continually evil all that bad? The entire temporal world is subject to corruption, subject to the wrath of God, and accordingly it and we, as temporal beings, are thoroughly evil. "For all our days pass away under thy wrath, our years come to an end like a sigh" (Ps. 90:9). Original sin is pervasive. And yet we ask questions and devise answers. We know that there are infinitely many prime numbers. Pleasures of the flesh are enjoyable. We rational, sentient beings love one another and experience the love of others. Born OK the first time? Hardly. But the condition or state of original sin, albeit continually evil—and continual because it is temporal—is complex. It is our state, as is the world. Now the latter may be ours in the same way that a prison cell belongs to the person incarcerated in it. But the prisoner, too, claims the cell to be his: the cot on which he sleeps, which could be softer but could also be harder; the toilet where he relieves himself, which could be cleaner but also could be dirtier. And it is in this world, our world, where we think and trust and love. To be sure, it is also the world where we err and betray and hate.

Time as perceived by us is sin. This assertion is in need of foundation, development, and expansion, but these must await another time and place. In this chapter my purposes were simply to address some of the questions and implications attending my postulate and to consider succession and especially entailment as substantial, i.e., as a-temporal. This I have deemed necessary in order to explore faith, which is necessarily temporal, in its relationship to the eternal. The relationship, I shall argue, is inherently contradictory and thereby anxious.

3

Kinds of Faith

To say what faith is exactly may be difficult or impossible, but faith surrounds and imbues our lives. We are creatures of faith, imperfect faith necessarily, whether we conceive our faith as condition or relationship, as a gift or a haunting. The description of faith developed here may seem bleak and dispiriting to some. It is all the more wondrous, then, that in the face of our own inattention, infidelities, and disavowals, we persist in our lives of faith. The unfaithful believe and expect to be trusted, because the unfaithful are the faithful.

We use the noun *faith* and the verb *to believe* in a variety of ways. Initially let me narrow the scope of *believe* to *believe in*, although even this restricted use can have a variety of meanings, such as *to think that something exists, to think with assent*, or *to trust something* or *someone*, i.e., to enter into a relationship with another person or thing, with the Other. In some cases it may be necessary to specify exactly who or what is believed, which may entail formulating an article of faith, a proposition. For example, to have faith in God usually means something different from having faith in one's lover. The former expression might entail solely a confidence that the object, God, no matter how vaguely conceived, is, exists, or acts. This narrow conception has a logical or analytical quality to it, especially if the object of faith lacks personality or personhood. The latter use of "have faith in," as in a lover, rarely means that the one who has faith is confident that the lover exists, although it may signify confidence that a particular person is indeed a lover. Confidence in the acting or being of God, however, usually demands much more than belief in acting or being, since the object itself, God, requires so much from us.

Here I use "object" loosely. The object of faith may be a lover, beauty, gold, reason, or God. But conceiving of God as a being may lead us astray. If not a being, then how can we possibly refer to God as an object? For Martin Buber, relation comes first and serves as cause of the *I* and *Thou* that appear as subjects and objects of the relationship. At least analytically, if not temporally, the individuals, *I* and *Thou*, are distinguished from each other and separated from the relationship itself only after the relationship has been established (Buber, *I and Thou* 27). Thus the object God is derived from a more primary encounter, one that has the character of trust. Paul Tillich, too, warns against conceiving of the object of faith as the object God who, because of his, her, or its absolute superiority, is rendered as a tyrant (*Courage* 170). By putting these two observations together I arrive at a common understanding of God, although it is the rejected God, i.e., the one to whom we, as subjects, have a victimized relationship. I shall persist in using the terms "being" and "object" to refer to God, in order to allow for a general discourse on faith, but I acknowledge both the complexity and imprecision of such use.

A relation of faith might also attribute fidelity to the object of faith rather than to the believer. Both Pope Francis and Karl Barth speak of the faithfulness of God, but this use of faith or faithfulness is more along the lines of trust: trust that gold will retain its value; trust that a lover will remain constant; trust that God cares for us and watches over us. Faithfulness on the part of the object of faith, therefore, may include many attributes and actions. These attributes may not in fact be predicated to the object of faith, but they are how the faithful person conceives of the object. Thus we might conceive of the LORD God as being both merciful and just without being able to reconcile the attributes, and accordingly we speak analogically. This sort of speech, our ability to draw analogies, is also an inability, because it does not speak to the being or essence of God. Augustine notes, for example, that "God's anger is not a disturbance of His mind" but rather a judgment, our description of the punishment incurred by sinfulness (*City of God* XV, 25).

Faith and faithfulness are not the same thing, although faithfulness may be an aspect of faith. We often read and hear that God and dogs are faithful. This means that they abide. They are trustworthy. One can count on them for certain things. But when we say that God is faithful, we do not mean that God has faith. God does not stand on the slippery rock of faith. We do.

I use faith to signify a temporal condition, a condition that in its theological use presupposes sin. Accordingly, God does not have faith. (No opinion about dogs is ventured in this regard.) And because of sin, faith presupposes the human being. Augustine claims that we can see our own faith. He thinks that we can see into our own hearts, that we can know ourselves at least with regard to faith (*De trinitate* XIII.1.3, 344). This assertion seems to be at odds with others made by Augustine that we are too distracted by the world in order to know ourselves.

I concur with Augustine's former position to the extent that the person of faith can see that he is exactly that, a person of faith, one who has the condition or is in fact haunted. But the person of faith is never at ease because the faith itself is always at risk. Only the sinner is a person of faith, but of course this person knows that he is a sinner. Indeed, sin is a qualification of faith, or at least for faith in God. (Something like vice is a qualification for other kinds of faith.) So what the person of faith sees, according to Augustine, must be something like intention. But here even the Apostle Paul acknowledges the fragile condition of good intentions: "For I do not do the good I want, but the evil I do not want is what I do" (Rom. 7:19).

I shall not attempt to provide my own definition of faith but avail myself of definitions made by others, especially those in the Letter to the Hebrews and by Augustine and Aquinas. These definitions are helpful starting points. We read in the Letter to the Hebrews (11:1): "Now faith is the assurance (or *substance*, ὑπόστασις) of things hoped for, the conviction (ἔλεγχος) of things not seen." In this definition, I understand hope in a very ordinary way to mean desire. For ὑπόστασις one might also read "foundation," "conviction," "confidence," or literally "standing under." Thus the first part of the definition becomes "assurance of things desired."

For the second part of the definition, one might read "testing," "certainty," or "verification" for ἔλεγχος. As for "things seen," it should be noted that to see commonly means to understand. Augustine and many others make explicit the connection of to see with to know or to understand, but the connection of seeing with knowing predates the Christian writers by many centuries (*Confessions* X.xxxv.54).

There are, of course, many more definitions of faith, but Buber develops an argument for there being only two types of faith, irrespective of the content and object of faith. The two types can be summarized as trusting and propositional. In one case, "I trust someone without being able to offer sufficient reasons for my trust in him." In the other case, again without giving reasons, "I acknowledge a thing to be true" (Buber, *Two Types of Faith* 7). As an example of the first type, Buber has in mind ancient Israel, including Jesus and his teachings as presented in the synoptic gospels, and their relationship to the God of Abraham. The second type is represented by Christianity and its theology as formulated by Paul. The proposition that is believed to be true is the resurrection of Jesus Christ (*Two Types of Faith* 9). Buber asserts that Paul in effect Hellenizes the message of Jesus by turning his teachings into a series of tenets, which eventually are acknowledged as a creed.

Much depends upon the someone who is trusted. Is this someone a person? Can it be thing-like such as beauty, reason, or gold? It would seem that propositions could be formed about the trust relationship, propositions that may be true or false. Both types of faith entail the uncertainty and struggle that I am inquiring about. The second, propositional type of faith, however, fits more neatly with the postulate concerning the eternality of God and his action. Buber seems to anticipate this aspect of faith, claiming that the trusting kind of faith has a temporal, albeit uncertain, beginning. But propositional faith concerns the truth which is acknowledged by the believer. Thus these two types of faith serve my inquiry, at least to the extent that they emphasize the distinction (and the union) of the temporal and the eternal. The first kind of faith points to the temporal: trust-ing. The second type appeals to the eternal.

Among the many objects of faith there are: gold, reason, the world, a lover, Dulcinea, God. These objects are truly separate, although Dulcinea verges on God. I take up reason and God together in order to distinguish between the two, a distinction hardly necessary in most cases, but also to respond to the notion that reason is not an object of faith. Although one might appeal to reason to assist in explaining what constitutes faith in God (Aquinas), most people would readily acknowledge that, for example, the God of Abraham is quite distinct from and even at times antagonistic to reason. In commenting on the promise of Isaac to Abraham, Luther claims that reason must be struck down or killed (*occidere*) for there to be faith (*Commentary on Galatians* 3:6; *Martin Luthers Werke* 40.1, 362). Elsewhere he refers to reason as the devil's whore. Barth provides a more explicit description: "[Faith] grips reason by the throat and strangles the beast" (*Epistle* 144). But neither is reason equivalent with the denial of God, a kind of denial that I call special atheism. Faith in reason is agnostic with respect to God, a supreme being, that which supremely is. I depend upon Augustine for this characterization of God and have already expressed wariness about using "being" in connection with this God, in order not to imply a being among beings. Augustine, aware of this danger, reverses the concern: "[God] is called being (*essentia*) truly and properly in such a way that perhaps only God ought to be called being" (*De trinitate* VII.5.10, 231). This is equivalent to the proposition that God is Being.

One might assert that, as an atheist, as a person who does not have faith in this God, he is relying solely on reason, and in so doing is not making a profession of faith. But what sort of ground is reason? To what or to whom does one appeal in order to make such a profession? Kant emphatically states at the beginning of his *Critique of Pure Reason* that atheism does not fall under the domain of reason: "Solely by means of critique can we cut off, at the very root, *materialism, fatalism, atheism*, freethinking, *lack of faith, fanaticism*, and *superstition*, which can become harmful universally ... [the] critique stands in contrast to *dogmatism*" (B xxxiv–xxxv; Preface, 34). In effect, Kant is pointing to competing gods, reason and the one of the Bible. These gods need compete only in terms of ultimate grounding. In fact, these exist practically side by side, that is, in the lives of human beings who worship at the temples of both gods. Practice is not theoretically clean and precise, and thus, when pressed to choose between the two, we often pick one while claiming something like agnosticism regarding the other. Crucial to my understanding of these two gods, reason and the God of Abraham, is that each requires belief on the part of the individual in order to be considered supreme and worthy of trust.

One might argue in favor of reason or the world that there can be no doubt about their existence, unlike the existence of God. But faith in God is not merely belief in the existence of something called God. Similarly, faith in reason or in the world is not mere belief in their existence. Faith entails a grounding—actually, it seeks grounding—that provides meaning and guidance for the human being. Thus the existence of reason or the world no more proves their trustworthiness than does the existence of a person prove his trustworthiness as a lover.

Many writers on faith (in God) attempt to reconcile faith with reason, from Augustine and Aquinas to modern writers like Paul Tillich. If these reconciliations are to be accepted, what do we make of Luther's remark? I offer here only a preliminary observation. The righteousness that Luther speaks of, that which was reckoned to Abraham owing to his faith, is independent of reason, even if reason provides some contingent arguments on behalf of faith. But Luther indicates a radical separation of faith and reason, not a subordinate role for reason. There are demands of faith, when articulated, that offend reason. These demands, especially the mixing of the eternal with the temporal epitomized by the Incarnation, will be developed at length in this book. Here I simply note that the person who professes a faith in God, in gold, or in a lover, almost invariably employs reason as a means to express his faith. This is so because the person is a person, a rational being with language. But the occasional opposition between faith in God and in reason (or in the world) is, strictly speaking, an opposition between equals to the extent that both God and reason are considered as objects of faith. The rational being is a being of reason, a being who grounds his faith in the unconditioned, in reason itself. Thus the rational being suffers the anxiety of faith in a way fundamentally no different from the person who believes in the God of Abraham. As Kant notes: "Reason, therefore, restlessly seeks the unconditionally necessary and sees itself compelled to assume this without having any means of making such necessity conceivable" (*Grounding* 62).

Let me also distinguish here between faith in the world and atheism in general. Faith in the world is entirely compatible with the denial of the God of Abraham, special atheism. But I doubt there is anyone who has no faith, no god whatsoever, a general atheist. We all have our gods, each of us more than one. When put on the spot, we often choose one at the expense of the others. But, in fact, we live divided, disintegrated lives. "I am scattered in times whose order I do not understand" (*Confessions* XI.xxix.39). This, in an odd way, is exactly what it means to be a person of faith. A person of faith contends, struggles, and fails. At one moment we believe in this god, at another moment in that god. Our external actions reveal our internal actions, not perfectly and not always, but sufficiently so to confirm our unsteadfastness.

Finally, a comment on the lover. When one speaks of faith in a lover, often the object of faith is constancy or fidelity, but this constancy is not some disembodied virtue. It is not the Good. One trusts the other person to remain faithful. One does not believe that the lover exists as a person but rather that that person in question is truly a lover. Here I attempt to be more explicit than Buber in his description of the type of faith that consists of trust in someone. The meaning of trust can be clarified. Exactly what constitutes faithful action and thought is less clear, but almost certainly sexual liaisons with others are prohibited.

In the example of lovers, let us consider the case where one of the pair is faithful in this very narrowly defined way—no sex with others—and the other is not. One heart has not been hardened, whereas the other heart has been hardened. One person believes, trusts, treats the other as an end in himself (Kant), and the other person treats the faithful one as a means. Why does one remain faithful while the other betrays? Was the gift given to both and subsequently taken away from one?

I have not sought to investigate the objects (gold, reason, etc.) themselves, but by way of anticipation I offer the following about the God-God. We might attribute personality or personhood to it, as in the case of Zeus or Athena. We might also attribute omniscience, omnipotence, omni-presence, and generation or creation: the omni-God. In the minds of some, we have now described a dictator, even if we were to include benevolence along with the other attributes. (The dictatorship or tyranny must result from the following reasoning. Things, the world, are a certain way. One could imagine them being different. For example, electrical and gravitational forces need not vary inversely nearly as the square of the distance. But things are the way they are, and accordingly we who have no choice in the matter are tyrannized by their being that way.) At least with respect to personality, this God or object differs from the others, and so let us call the God-God the person-God, or on occasion the eternal actor. Stripping out personality from eternal actor produces eternal action. The person-God deserves special comment.

He, He. He! We can replace "He" with "She" or "Thou" but not with "It." Much is made of the biblical passage regarding the creation of man: "So God created man in his own image, ...

male and female he created them" (Gen. 1:26-7). Connected with this creation is dominion and reproduction. From this passage it is common to derive an image of God made in the likeness of man. That a god, the gods, God be conceived with personality is hardly unique to the Hebrew bible. These are gods to whom one speaks. Even Augustine, who seems in certain places to have an understanding of the eternal, timeless God, speaks to God and prays to God in the form of the psalms throughout his *Confessions*. Augustine acknowledges, however, that "person" does violence in a way to the God that is supremely. Regarding the trinity, he claims that "person" is an attempt to answer the question "Three what?" "So human inadequacy searched for a word to express three what, and it said substances (*substantiae*) or persons (*personae*)" (*De trinitate* VII.4.9, 230). We are left, then, with an image of a mask, the persona through which the actor speaks. Whoever or whatever the actor may be, he, she, or it appears behind the mask, but the language used is one that we understand, at least superficially. We see the mask and imagine it speaking.

This is a God with whom one forms a relationship. This is a God with whom one deals as persons deal with one another, mutually (*I and Thou* Postscript, 6:135). Buber acknowledges that we do not know God's essence, a matter explicated at length by Aquinas. But Aquinas defends the application of names to God. We know God, indirectly, from creatures, from creation, and we know God *as* creatures. Accordingly, we name God (*Summa theologica* I, Q.13, A.1). One sees evidence, perhaps, of God in creation, but one does not see God. Paul writes: "Ever since the creation of the world his invisible nature, namely, his eternal power and deity, has been clearly perceived in the things that have been made" (Rom. 1:20). One sees the butterfly or the rainbow. What does one perceive clearly (καθοράω)? We perceive our own wonder about the butterfly or rainbow. Is this an image of God? We do not know God.

The skeptic might claim that all gods, if they have personhood, are necessarily made in the image of man. Even revelation is of little help since it must reveal in terms that are understood by man. Thus, if God is revealed or discovered to be a person, he will have the characteristics of a human being. He may be vengeful, just, merciful, loving. He may hear our prayer or turn his back on us. Even the biblical God, who becomes increasingly remote and spiritualized throughout the Hebrew Bible, who claims his name is "I Am Who I Am" (Exod. 3:14), appears in the Greek Bible as the Father.

In the Hebrew Bible we encounter similes for God, e.g., lion (Hos. 11:10) and strong tower (Prov. 18:10), and there is the intimate and personal conversation of the Psalms and Isaiah. In Exodus alone we read about the hand, nostrils, finger, face of God who is like a man, a friend (3:20, 7:5, 15:3,15:8, 31:18, 33:11). Even with our very example from Exodus (3:14), we have a LORD that refers to him-/her-/itself as "I." Indeed, we have a LORD not *that* refers but *who* refers to himself as "I." Who or what says "I?" A person.

We are finite and limited, so our names for God render him finite and limited. Thus we praise and blaspheme in the same utterance. According to Buber, in contradictory terms we are calling upon the absolute person (*I and Thou* 6:136). Later, I shall take up again the personhood of this God as well as its implications for idolatry. At this point, let me simply state that much of this study issues forth from an inquiry into the Eternal I, the seemingly paradoxical person who is a-temporal, but now I return to kinds of faith and corresponding gods.

All of these gods are widely worshipped. Most people worship more than one of these gods, and some of us worship all of them. One may wonder how someone can worship the world along with any of the others, for example, the person-God. In the Sermon on the Mount, Jesus says: "No one can serve two masters; for either he will hate the one and love the other, or he will be devoted to the one and despise the other. You cannot serve God and mammon" (Mt. 6:24). This remark serves as refuge for those who do not wish to deal with the complexity of the matter at hand. If life and its decisions were constructed in a strict and clearly perceived hierarchy, then perhaps the claim would make sense. But life is more complicated than that, and we all serve many masters. Sometimes the many masters seem to come into conflict. At the very least, we often encounter trouble discerning the boundaries of jurisdiction among the gods. Even in a monolithic structure, an inferior must decide whether to serve and obey his immediate superior or his superior's superior.

One cannot serve all the gods without conflict and inconsistency. This is seen most clearly in the person-God/world-god opposition. Jesus was referring, I presume, to the opposition of the person-God, whom he claims to be his father, and the expanded and more general conception of the gold-god. And yet some faith to all the gods is possible and even common.

Although the argument forthcoming is not intended to be essentially a psychological one, it will be based on human beings living in this world, moving from moment to moment. My entire inquiry is founded on this inconsistency, this existence, this life. Faith, as conceived here, is a condition of sinners, a condition of disintegrated souls. These human beings are bound by time, and yet they seek, at the very least, to approach the eternal, to touch it. Reflecting upon these inconsistencies, one often feels forced into a general claim of agnosticism. Is agnosticism any more than momentary forgetfulness? What can we know about our own belief?

Some of the faith objects, gold in particular, seem to be more a means than an end. The investor in gold may have ulterior motives other than worship of the metal itself. I believe that such ulterior motives can be ascribed to all apparent declarations of faith. With these considerations I find prudence entering into the deliberations, and accordingly wonder if such a practical virtue has a role in the faith relationship. Is a person of faith concerned about means and ends? Our prudence is unavoidable. We find it even in the religious zealot. Some might see it as evidence of original sin. Our calculations of how to achieve our ends are worldly indeed, even when these ends seem to be other worldly. This is an inquiry into faith in this world, the only kind of faith known to us. And when we elevate the world to godly status, then our prudence seems all the more appropriate.

As interesting or worthy as the other gods may be, the vast majority of these remarks concern directly the person-god, in particular the God-God or omni-God of the Old and New Testaments. In developing these thoughts, I have attempted to keep all the gods in mind. Many of these observations could be extended with some modifications to deal specifically with each. In treating the omni-God or eternal actor as an object of faith, however, we shall encounter some unique characteristics that may require unique means, even if they are characteristics peculiar to us humans. For example, if this God demands ultimate concern from the person of faith, as the First Commandment seems to indicate, then polytheism is explicitly forbidden. In contrast, one can imagine a person confessing faith both in gold and in reason, even while acknowledging that the two objects may come into conflict in certain circumstances.

Faith in the omni-God, however, may be similar to faith in the gold-god in that the expression of faith may be motivated by concerns other than pure adoration. I just noted that the ultimate concern of the person who believes in gold in many cases may be more aptly described as preservation of purchasing power. Similarly, faith in the person-God may be motivated primarily by a desire for happiness, the hope that the God will in some way ultimately insure the happiness of the person of faith. This motivation does not appear to be pure adoration. Perhaps a somewhat more elevated desire would be recognition as faithful. Don Quixote claims that knights errant serve their ladies expecting nothing in return except that their service be accepted. Sancho replies that he has heard preachers say the same thing about loving Our Lord, but that he prefers to serve for what he can get in return (Cervantes, *Don Quijote* I.31, 252–3). Might not this be a suitable reward for faith: mere acknowledgment by the object of faith that the person is faithful? Nothing more. In a way, this is what Ahab sought and received from the whale.

This consideration of gods has been motivated by kinds of faith, which faith is variously defined as assurance, substance, conviction, testing, gift, relation, and curse. With particular reference to the omni-God, I add Tillich's courage to the definition of relation:

> Since the relation of man to the ground of his being must be expressed in symbols taken from the structure of being, the polarity of participation and individualization determines the special character of this relation as it determines the special character of the courage to be. If participation is dominant, the relation to being-itself has a mystical character, if individualization prevails the relation to being-itself has a personal character, if both poles are accepted and transcended the relation to being itself has the character of faith. (*Courage* 144–5)

Heidegger kneels at this altar.

Tillich's faith, although perhaps lacking in special content, is narrowly directed toward the God above God. As such, this faith is only an instance of the kinds of faith that are under consideration here. But even faith in the omni-God seeks content. This content is knowledge or wisdom. Aquinas claims that "God, Who is pure act without any admixture of potentiality, is in Himself supremely knowable" (*Summa theologica* I, Q.12, A.1). We creatures, of course, are incapable of knowing God in this way. Thus we must inquire into the relationship between the objective and the object.

4

Faith as Pursuit of Knowledge

In order to understand better what faith is, let us first consider the objective of faith. Here I distinguish between objective and object, although in a sense they may be the same. Rather than the person-God, Dulcinea, or the world, I seek the purpose for believing. What does the believer seek? Does the believer have a choice whether or not to believe? Following Don Quixote's example, I have already suggested that a reward for faith is that the person of faith be acknowledged as such, that the lady accept the service of the knight, resulting in justification or righteousness. But the notion of reward indicates a return on investment, quid pro quo. My concern here is narrower, restricted to the immediate purpose of faith. I am not speaking about the next life.

The person of faith wants to know the object of faith. The person wants "the assurance of things hoped for." This desire amounts to an annihilation of faith. The investor wants to know that gold will retain its value. Certainly, it is knowledge that his service has been accepted that the knight seeks from the lady, that which Don Quixote never received from Dulcinea but which Ahab in a way received from the whale. Even Buber's pre-Hellenic Jew wants to know, to be certain of the Lord whom he trusts, even if he does not formulate a proposition to that effect.

In *Confessions*, Augustine repeatedly states his desire for knowledge, certainty, and wisdom. He wants to be as certain regarding things he could not see as he was about $7 + 3 = 10$ (*Confessions* VI.iv.6). Regarding his vision at Ostia with his mother, he writes: "Eternal life is of the quality of that moment of understanding after which we sighed" (*Confessions* IX.xi.25), and later: "May I know you who know me" (*Confessions* X.i.1). I agree with these remarks and conclude that to know is good.

The investor, Don Quixote, Ahab, and the pre-Hellenic Jew want to know something about the object, gold, Dulcinea, the whale, and the LORD. Augustine seeks understanding, perhaps about everything, but he voices this desire as one in which he wants to know God: "May I know you."

In a commentary on the Gospel of John (17:14-18), Augustine offers the following summary of his desire: "Do you wish to understand (*intellegere*)? Believe. For God has said by the prophet: Unless you believe, you shall not understand [Isa. 7:9] ... For understanding is the reward of faith. Therefore do not seek to understand in order to believe, but believe that you may understand; since, except ye believe, you shall not understand" (*Homilies on John* 29.6; see also *De trinitate* VII.4.12, 236 and XV.2.3, 396). In Augustine's thinking, this knowing and understanding will be the culmination of faith (see also *City of God* XXII.29).

Augustine's notion is adopted by Anselm in the preface to his *Proslogium*, where he writes: "I have written the following treatise, in the person of one who strives to lift his mind to the contemplation of God, and seeks to understand what he believes" (*Proslogium* 2). The original title of the *Proslogium* was "Faith Seeking Understanding."

"Unless you believe, you shall not understand." A more common translation of Isaiah 7:9 is: "If you will not believe, surely you shall not be established." Pope Francis addresses this apparent mistranslation. (Augustine was aware of this discrepancy, see *On Christian Doctrine* II.12.) He points to a play on words between "to believe" and "to be established" (Francis, *Lumen fidei* 23). Adopting a framework similar to Buber's two kinds of faith, Francis acknowledges that Augustine's words seem to move from trust in the original to a proposition in the Latin translation. Francis asserts, however, that the firm foundation offered by Isaiah's "established" is grounded in an understanding of God and his relationship to our lives. Thus he sees a dialogue between Judaism and Hellenism, one in which Augustine synthesizes "understanding" with "being established." The English speaker is further tempted to associate the standing of understanding with the standing of establish. Both understanding and establish seek to fix firmly, to grasp and hold tightly in place. Thus belief has as its end the firm fixing in place.

One might think that Buber's first type of faith, trust in someone, would not be a quest for knowledge. Certainly, the momentary and often emotional sense and expression of faith seem to be far removed from understanding. We might even consider an infant's reliance on and trust of its mother as a limited example of this first type. The infant's trust may be instinctual, but in that respect it may be seen as a widely and generously bestowed gift, just as faith is often claimed to be a gift.

In the Evangelist John's rendition of the Last Supper, Jesus instructs his disciples regarding their future life after he has departed. He speaks of the Counsellor whom he will send, and then puzzles his listeners with the remark: "A little while, and you will see me no more; again a little while, and you will see me" (Jn 16:16). Jesus attempts to assuage their concerns, and notes: "I have said this to you in figures; the hour is coming when I shall no longer speak to you in figures but tell you plainly of the Father" (Jn 16:25). Jesus continues to speak of his relationship with the Father, and the disciples respond that Jesus is now speaking plainly, not in figures. John continues:

> When Jesus had spoken these words, he lifted up his eyes to heaven and said, "Father, the hour has come; glorify thy Son that the Son may glorify thee, since thou hast given him power over all flesh, to give eternal life (αἰώνιος ζωή) to all whom thou hast given him. And this is eternal life, that they may know (γινώσκωσιν) thee the only true God, and Jesus Christ whom thou hast sent." (Jn 17:1-3)

In my interpretation here, eternal is the word to be taken literally, whereas life is metaphorical. Before addressing the temporal aspect of faith, however, let us consider it as knowledge. Even interpreted as a way of life, faith is equated with knowledge. "Keep [the statutes] and do them; for that will be your wisdom and your understanding in the sight of the peoples, who, when they hear all these statutes, will say, 'Surely this great nation is a wise and understanding people'" (Deut. 4:6).

In the Gospel of John, Jesus has finally spoken plainly about eternal life, the accomplishment of faith. The reward, or more properly the goal, is knowledge. Strictly speaking, this is not a knowledge that is achieved after a life of faith, a reward received in the next life. The knowledge, if it truly is eternal, does not have essentially a temporal context, although temporal beings such as we may have a kind of access to it. Thus the reward of faith is unlike other rewards.

The promise of faith is further echoed in Paul's famous lines: "For now we see in a mirror dimly, but then face to face. Now I know in part; then I shall understand fully, even as I have been fully understood" (1 Cor. 13:12). And in his letter to the Ephesians, Paul claims that the gifts of Christ build "up the body of Christ, until we all attain to the unity of the faith and of the knowledge of the Son of God, to mature manhood, to the measure of the stature of the fullness of Christ" (Eph. 4:12-13). This maturity, the objective of faith, is a standing, not collectively with Christ, but as one, fixed, established. The new nature put on by the follower of Christ is a means to understanding. "Do not lie to one another, seeing that you have put off the old nature with its practices and have put on the new nature, which is being renewed in knowledge after the image of the creator" (Col. 3:9-10). Thus the faithful will see, i.e., know and understand Jesus as the Son of God. "Knowledge of the Son of God" is exactly what Jesus had promised. John Calvin concurs: "Faith consists in knowledge (*cognitio*) of God and divine will ... explicit recognition of the divine goodness" (*Institutes* III.2; S.2, 356).

I acknowledge the disparity between some of the expressions used by these authors and my insistence on an eternal reward. We read about "now and then," "maturity," "promise." These all seem to point to a future. We are temporal beings and we think and speak accordingly. But I maintain that the knowledge or understanding sought does not have a future existence. The future that Augustine, Paul, and John speak of is not in the future.

Faith itself, rather than the promise of faith, is often described as a kind of knowledge. Aquinas calls it a mean between science and opinion (*Summa theologica* II.ii, Q.1, A.2). On behalf of the object known, i.e., believed in, if that object is the person-God, the knowledge of faith is superior to ordinary human knowledge because it derives its certainty from the perfection of the thing known or believed in.

Augustine draws a distinction between knowledge (*scientia*) and wisdom (*sapientia*). Knowledge refers to worldly facts and events. Wisdom concerns the truth, that which is eternal, "and it is the contemplation of this that makes us happy or blessed" (*De trinitate* XIII.1.2, 343). The "knowledge" promised by Jesus, eternal life, falls into both categories on Augustine's account. That one "may know thee the only true God" is a matter of contemplation and wisdom. But that one may know "Jesus Christ whom thou hast sent" falls into both categories. Jesus Christ as the Word is eternal and a subject of wisdom or contemplation. But "the Word made flesh, which is Christ Jesus, has treasures both of wisdom and of knowledge," because an empirical, historical, and contingent fact is combined with eternal truth (*De trinitate* XIII.19.24, 366).

Thus the knowledge sought by faith and offered by Jesus is of a special sort. Calvin distinguishes this knowledge (*cognitio*) from human comprehension (*comprehensio*). The knowledge of faith far surpasses that kind of understanding or comprehension of which the human mind is capable, so much so that the human being can only feel persuaded by it (*Institutes* III.2; S.14, 364). By "comprehension" Calvin must mean something like understanding, the "reason" that Luther claims must be killed or beaten to the ground. The Incarnation is an affront to our understanding.

Regarding the certitude of faith, Aquinas asserts that certainty about something is directly related to its cause. Thus the knowledge of faith in God becomes supremely knowable owing to its source. But it is not supremely knowable by us. From the creature's point of view, knowing something by means of our intellect is more certain than faith "because the matters of faith are above the human intellect" (*Summa theologica* II.ii, Q.4, A.8). The wisdom that Aquinas refers to differs from that of Augustine and, being founded on human reason, likely includes experience and prudence.

Aquinas would seem to be describing a faith at odds with the one being developed here, since he attributes certainty to faith. But the certainty is attributable to the cause of faith, the source of the condition. And perhaps by grace the individual, the recipient of the condition, or curse (we *fall* in love), may participate in this certainty. But the person of faith is temporal, uncertain, and in search of the fixity that we call knowledge. Thus, in order to align with the object of faith, if the object is the person-God, the believer must attain to a superhuman level of knowledge. This level is superhuman in that it surpasses existence. It is eternal, a-temporal.

On behalf of the knower or believer, therefore, the knowledge is less certain than ordinary human knowledge, even factual or temporalized knowledge. Factual or temporalized knowledge can be doubted. Did Caesar really cross the Rubicon? It would seem that some knowledge, say of the mathematical sort, when truly understood by the knower, cannot be doubted, at least not in all sincerity. Consider, for example, Aristotle's remarks about incommensurability presented in Chapter 2. In opposition to this position, if one insists on and truly believes along with Heidegger that all being is temporalized, then presumably all knowledge of being is also temporalized and subject to doubt. "A skeptic can no more be refuted than the Being of truth can be 'proved'" (*Being and Time* H229).

The knowledge of faith, if it can at all be called knowledge, is of a decidedly different sort. Aquinas argues that only the object of faith in God constitutes man's genuine happiness. Only God can completely satisfy the will and the intellect of man. Only God can make man perfectly happy (*Summa theologica* II.i, Q.2, A.8). Regardless of whatever "will," "intellect," "knowledge," and "happiness" may mean, according to Aquinas only the knowledge of God, the end of faith, leaves man in the eternally blessed state: knowing.

Aquinas also argues that man's created intellect can see the essence of God, that is, it can know God. Things (broadly understood) are knowable to the extent that they are actual, and God is pure act. There is no potential in God. Therefore God is perfectly knowable, but this perfect knowledge is perfect in God's perspective, so to speak. Man's highest faculty is his intellect, and since all creation is purposive, man has an intellect for a reason, i.e., to be used. Thus, in seeing God, man employs his intellect to its greatest extent. The end of man is his happiness, and this happiness is perfected in the vision (knowledge) of God. Aquinas argues further that the blessed state is suggested by nature itself (intimation of Rom. 1:19-20). Naturally, man desires to know. Only a haphazard creation, or worse, a perverse creation, would consist of a natural desire that could not be satisfied under any circumstances (*Summa theologica* II.i, Q.2, A.1).

Thus Aquinas assumes: (1) that man has an end or purpose; (2) man's end is happiness or beatitude; (3) man's highest faculty is his intellect; (4) man's happiness consists in the use or fulfillment of his highest faculty. Man's creator, the truth, intended for man that he know the truth. According to Aquinas, we are not dealing with a perverse or ironic object of faith, an object that creates and elicits a desire that cannot be satisfied. In fact, all of creation is ordered and hierarchal. Of course, this state of blessedness is necessarily unattainable in this life. Aquinas writes that God is "pure act," a claim that corresponds to use here of "eternal actor" or "eternal action" as one of the designations for the omni-God, a designation that emphasizes both the timelessness of God as well as the timeless action of consequence or logical entailment. In further arguing that one intellect may see the essence of God more perfectly than another (*Summa theologica* I, Q.12, A.6), Aquinas cites the very passage from John's Gospel that I am using (17:3). Much to the annoyance of Hobbes, who finds the expression "unintelligible" (*Leviathan* 6, 130), Aquinas calls this knowing, this eternal life, the beatific vision (*Summa theologica* III, Supplement, Q.92).

There are different kinds of knowledge, and we must inquire into what kind of knowledge, promised by Jesus (Jn 17:3), is entailed by the beatific vision. Rather than embarking on a rigorous inquiry into epistemology, I proceed by analogy.

There is factual knowledge, or, more narrowly, historical knowledge or knowledge that will become historical. This knowledge is temporal in its nature; it concerns an event or happening. Kierkegaard calls it approximation (*Postscript* 21). Augustine distinguishes it from wisdom, contemplation of the eternal. This knowledge may be expressed as a proposition, or as a declarative sentence. Examples of this kind of knowledge include the following:

1. Caesar crossed the Rubicon.
2. Tomorrow is Saturday.
3. Thomas Jefferson was the second president of the United States.

If one were to assume that time is truly independent, i.e., that time is practically separate from space and that certain truths or entities such as numbers are completely free of time, then factual knowledge could be considered as dependent upon time for its veracity. Facts would be events. Even the fact of sensation presupposes time.

Another kind of knowledge is necessary for logical entailment: consequence. In Euclid's *Elements*, time does not separate the postulates from the Pythagorean Theorem, but logical order establishes the predecessor and successor, the antecedent and the consequent as such.

Our understanding of equality or sameness may provide evidence of another kind of non-temporal knowledge. We understand what it means for two things to be the same or to be equal, just as we understand what it means for them to be different or unequal. This understanding is coupled with our ability to discern between two things. In other words, when we say that two things are equal or the same, usually what we mean is that we can discern between two things and that we see the ways in which they are the same. Of course, we make mistakes of identity all the time, but each such mistake is verification for our understanding of equality and sameness. This kind of knowledge seems to be more primitive than knowledge of logical entailment, more like knowledge of numbers and succession than knowledge of necessary consequence and cause and effect. These latter two kinds, equality and entailment, unlike historical knowledge, do not consort with time, although the understanding of equality, discerning same and different, is applied by us temporally.

Now consider the knowledge promised by Jesus as eternal life. Those who have it "know thee the only true God." The beatific vision is eternal, outside of or independent of time. It is Augustine's wisdom. We may be able to say very little about this knowledge, presumably this highest and greatest and perfect of all knowing, other than it is eternal, outside of time. We human beings, finite and temporal, are capable of at least a presentiment or glimpse of such knowledge. The evidence for this comes from our capacity to think logically and mathematically. We must acknowledge, however, that the knowledge is beheld by temporally bound beings. Temporality is lurking in "glimpses."

That such knowledge constitutes our greatest happiness is argued by many, from Augustine to Kierkegaard. And yet the happy or blessed aspect of this knowledge is curious and may be even foreign to many of our instincts since it seems to reduce the knowledge of the only true God to something like knowledge of the syllogism.

Those who have this knowledge, according to John 17:3, also know "Jesus Christ whom thou hast sent." Knowing Jesus Christ seems to be, at least in part, historical knowledge, knowledge that is both temporal and contingent. Knowledge of the Incarnation, although infinitely rich in significance and meaning, is also nonsense. (The Incarnation is related to my postulate in Chapter 1. I shall, on occasion, apply this term *corollary* to the Incarnation, since it follows from the postulate. The corollary does not prove the postulate. Similarly, effects may entail a cause but they do not prove the cause, at least not a particular cause. A corollary might, however, add interest or significance, if not plausibility, to the postulate. Thus the corollary of the Incarnation follows from the postulate but not necessarily so. All corollaries are necessary consequences of the propositions to which they are attached. But the necessity of their consequence speaks only to their possibility. The proposition makes the corollary possible. Thus the postulate, as I understand it, makes the Incarnation possible, as I understand it.)

Knowledge of the Incarnation is the eternal truth or significance of an historical event. This is the knowledge of the living God. (In a way, God the Father is not living. God the Father does not exist.) Jesus confirms this interpretation in asserting: "I am the way, and the truth, and the life; no one comes to the Father, but by me. If you had known me, you would have known my Father also; henceforth you know him and have seen him" (Jn 14:6-7). The Incarnation provides partial argument or evidence for the contradictory answer in Chapter 2 to the question "Is Time? Yes *and* no."

The Evangelist John emphasizes the mystery of the Incarnation as he reports a conversation between Jesus and his friend Martha regarding her brother Lazarus who had died.

> Jesus said to her, "I am the resurrection and the life; he who believes in me, though he die, yet shall he live, and whoever lives and believes in me shall never die. Do you believe this?" She said to him, "Yes, Lord; I believe that you are the Christ, the Son of God, he who is coming into the world." (Jn 11:25-7)

Martha uses the middle progressive participle, "who is coming" (ἐρχόμενος) into the world, to emphasize the complexity of the event. She is not referring to an event in the future. Jesus is standing before her in the world. Neither is she referring to an event in the past or an event that might be thought of as completed, which would require the aorist participle. Martha does not say "I believe that you are the Christ who has come into the world." In her response, Martha does not refer to the birth of Jesus.

The Incarnation is an example of transcendence. It contains both the eternal and the contingent. We can imagine the birth of Jesus but we cannot imagine the Incarnation. Augustine writes about how we can imagine the face of Jesus, and that our images will differ from one another, although Jesus of Nazareth had but one face. But Augustine emphasizes that these images do not, in a way, pertain to faith (*De trinitate* VIII.4.7, 248). By this Augustine means that we can imagine the birth of a baby boy, and can imagine that boy growing into manhood. We can imagine the man Jesus, perhaps with long, flowing, brown hair and a beard. But we cannot imagine the Son of God become man. Thus, in a way, all Christian painting and sculpture is idolatry.

I have been trying to describe the roles played by the intellect, the understanding, and the imagination in encountering or taking up the eternal. The imagination, rooted in our spatial and temporal intuitions, is stopped short. The understanding, thinking without pictures, may be able to go further. But however limited our faculties may be, and however contextualized may be our faith, the primary goal or aim of faith remains to know.

Thus there is ample testimony for knowledge as a reward or result of faithfulness. How successful one might be in this life in acquiring the knowledge sought by faith is another matter entirely. Karl Barth is especially dubious about such attainment. He goes so far as to claim, in apparent opposition to Romans 1:19-20, that the power of God cannot be detected in nature (*Epistle* 36). "For all alike [faith] is a scandal, a hazard … for all it is a leap into the void" (*Epistle* 99). According to Barth, Jesus Christ, the Son of God, is almost entirely unknowable. Thus even the second part of eternal life as defined by Jesus, "to know Jesus Christ whom thou hast sent," seems remote. The potter and the clay are incommensurable (*Epistle* 356). In fact, the person of faith is in a perpetual state of ignorance.

It may be worth drawing a distinction regarding in which ways God or Jesus Christ are known. Aquinas and Calvin have already argued for the certainty of faith in God when viewed or considered from the object of faith. If the object is the truth, then faith in that object is in a way absolutely certain, but certain from the side of the object. From the side of the believer, however, faith is a struggle that always falls short of the certainty of knowledge. Analogous to this distinction, in a reverse way, is the knowledge of God that Barth writes about. Certainly, man knows nothing whatsoever of God when considered from the side of God—we do not know his essence—and perhaps nearly nothing of Jesus Christ when considered from the side of the Son of God made man. This is Barth's argument. The only part of Jesus Christ that we can know is the part that we call Jesus of Nazareth, the part that Augustine invites us to imagine. But by means of revelation, by signs, man comes to know about God and about Jesus Christ, although this knowledge necessarily is human knowledge. One might even call it *hearsay*. Were it not for revelation of some sort, we would err in even referring to the essence of God. It takes a kind of faith to posit God's essence.

Barth uses geometric metaphors that may be helpful in understanding the problem of knowledge that he emphasizes. He writes: "The name Jesus defines an historical occurrence and marks the point where the unknown world cuts the known world." And: "As Christ, Jesus is the plane which lies beyond our comprehension. The plane which is known to us, He intersects vertically, from above. Within history, Jesus as the Christ can be understood only as Problem or Myth" (*Epistle* 29–30).

I shall develop the image. Let all of human knowledge and experience, both actual and potential, be represented by a plane. Jesus of Nazareth exists in this plane as a line segment. Let Jesus Christ be a plane, as suggested by Barth, or a surface that intersects the plane of human knowledge and experience in a line. This line contains the segment designated as Jesus of Nazareth. We can imagine the line of intersection extending indefinitely in both directions because we can think of time extending indefinitely into the past or into the future. Accordingly, we assign to the portions of the line beyond the segment our thought of Jesus before and after he lived. But we have no knowledge of the plane or surface that produces the line other than by means of the line of intersection. Our access to Christ, then, is through Jesus, and our human access is limited to the man Jesus. Without revelation, we know nothing about that which cuts our plane. For example, we cannot tell if the cut is made by a plane or by a curved surface. Indeed, knowledge may be too elevated a term for what we have, which in reality is simply a report, hearsay. Calvin writes that the human mind "feels" the knowledge and is persuaded (*Institutes* III.2; S.14, 364). Other writers call this grace.

From this report, from the promise made by Jesus at John 17:3, some men boldly proclaim that God lives and they speak of a living God. This living is reflected in the expression "eternal life" so often employed by Jesus. In this chapter I have considered eternal to be literal (in my sense) whereas life was taken to be metaphorical, and I have gone so far as to entertain the notion that God neither lives nor exists. Now let us ask about the metaphor. Just as one is puzzled by the Incarnation, the creator become creature, the eternal become temporal, so is one equally puzzled by the opposite movement, life become eternal.

Life is good. At the end of the First Letter of John, the author states: "And this is the testimony, that God gave us eternal life, and this life is in his Son. He who has the Son has life; he who has not the Son of God has not life" (1 Jn 5:11-12). This is the line of thought that leads to claims about the living God. The risen Christ signals the victory over death, which is the enemy of life. The wages of sin have been repaid once and for all. But life is temporal, it entails time. Thus, strictly speaking, life cannot be eternal. Either eternal or life must be taken metaphorically or analogically, and I have taken the latter as such. We have here two instances of nonsense, reflections of each other. One is life eternal and the other is God alive. Our understanding of life entails both time and death. A God who lives is a God who dies.

At this point, we can safely say that faith as the pursuit of knowledge comes at a price; it is a struggle. Faith without doubt is not faith, just as courage without fear is not courage. Calvin notes that we on earth "are still pilgrims ... [and] many things are hidden from us ... In all men faith is always mingled with incredulity" (*Institutes* III.2, S.4, 357). The person of faith struggles perpetually with distrust, so much so that "the minds of believers are seldom at rest" (*Institutes* III.2, S.17 and 37, 366–7 and 379). Thus the "assurance" (ὑπόστασις) and "conviction" (ἔλεγχος) in the definition of faith found in the Letter to the Hebrews are constantly under assault. The testing aspect of ἔλεγχος comes to the fore. The necessarily temporal character of faith manifests itself as tension. Therefore the knowledge sought by faith is unattainable in this life, because the knowledge per se is not of the temporal sort, but it is sought in a temporal mode.

Faith entails trust in the object of faith. What the person of faith, the believer, wants is assurance, knowledge. This knowledge may not be identical to the activity of the intellect implied by the beatific vision, "the ultimate beatitude of man," but the two are related. What the person of faith wants, however, is exactly what he is denied. He wants to know the object. But the faith relation requires that the person of faith remain true to the object while simultaneously and at every moment being denied his desire, knowledge. The redeemed sinner temporally remains a sinner. The "new man" of Paul's letters remains the "old man." This denial produces anxiety. Faith is ironic, because, strictly speaking, there are no rewards for perfect faith. One receives absolutely nothing in exchange for placing one's faith in the faith object, the person-God, a lover, the world. In this regard, the story of Abraham and Isaac is paradigmatic.

The LORD said to Abraham: "Take your son, your only son Isaac, whom you love, and go to the land of Moriah, and offer him there as a burnt offering upon one of the mountains of which I shall tell you" (Gen. 22:2). The LORD did not offer a deal to Abraham. He did not say: "You give me back Isaac, and I'll make your descendants as numerous as the stars" (see Gen. 15:5-6). The LORD had already promised that to Abraham. The LORD offered absolutely nothing in exchange for Isaac, nor did the LORD provide justification for his command. He did not say to Abraham: "Give me your most cherished possession for the following reason." There is no exchange here, no quid pro quo. Faith is blind to justice. Is it any wonder that it leads to anxiety.

This analysis is good as far as it goes. But the trial of Abraham was not a free-standing event, clinically sealed off from the life of Abraham. Abraham and the LORD had a history, one that even included negotiations over the fate of Sodom and Gomorrah (Gen. 18:22-33). Abraham had already seen what the LORD could do, had witnessed his might as well as his generosity. In short, Abraham had reason to trust the LORD. This is not to claim that he had sufficient reason to attempt to sacrifice Isaac. That act does shine brightly as the paragon of faith, but it is a single act.

Like Abraham, the person of faith has some experience that fosters his faith. This experience may be dwarfed by the demands of faith to the point of insignificance, eternally speaking. Nonetheless, there are temporal events and signs (revelation) that promote faithfulness. Could it be that some rewards of faith may be obtained piecemeal, just as faith itself must have its foundation in finite, temporal events and actions? These events and actions, individually or cumulatively, may be inadequate to produce faith even the size of a mustard seed. Two individuals may witness the same occurrence, a so-called miracle, and have different reactions, i.e., have different beliefs about the occurrence. But no one has faith based on absolutely no evidence, no sign, no revelation whatsoever. And so might not there be a more complex way in which faith is instilled and preserved?

Let us now turn our attention to the aspect of belief in faith. Regardless of how one characterizes faith, it involves the act of belief. Even the faithfulness of God or of a lover is a matter of belief for the one beloved. As has been noted, the experience of trust in someone or something may not seem immediately to be propositional, to be in the form of a declaration. One might even consider trust in certain circumstances to be instinctual. Thus neither the intellect nor the will may appear, at least superficially, to be part of such a belief. Certainly, a third party, an observer, could formulate a proposition to express the condition of trust or faithfulness. *A* believes *B*, by which is meant that *A* trusts *B*. *A* may not be able to articulate the tenets of a creed. Such ignorance or innocence, as we shall see, does not enable *A* to avoid the anxiety that accompanies the faith relationship.

Perhaps a more conventional notion of belief—of *to believe*—is to hold something as true. Aquinas addresses this kind of belief when he, relying on Augustine's definition, asks: "Whether To Believe Is To Think With Assent?" (*Summa theologica* II.ii, Q.2, A.1). Aquinas considers belief as a combination of separate operations or faculties, the intellect and the will. If belief is thinking with assent, then belief entails the intellectual faculty in that the believer thinks a thought. But belief, on this account, also entails the will in that the believer assents to the thought.

Aquinas, following Augustine, focuses on thinking that entails inquiry and deliberation. He identifies thinking that results in firm assent as science, and the thinker understands what is or has been thought. Some acts of the intellect conclude in doubt, inclining neither to one side or the other. Here Aquinas seems to be assuming a simple, two-fold possibility, either assent or denial. Thus he assumes that the thought is a proposition that has the character or appearance of being true or false. In contrast to these kinds of thinking there is belief. "But this act, *to believe*, cleaves firmly to one side, in which respect belief has something in common with science and understanding; yet its knowledge does not attain the perfection of clear vision, wherein it agrees with doubt, suspicion and opinion" (*Summa theologica* II.ii, Q.2, A.1).

Are matters really this straightforward? Is the will a separate faculty from the thinking intellect, and how does it operate? Are the objects of faith propositions which are either true or false? We know that self-referential statements can pose a problem here. For our purposes the following statement will suffice. "This statement is false." The truth or falsity of the statement is questionable, perhaps paradoxical, and at least contextual. Self-referential statements seem to be a trick. I cite the "liar paradox" merely to indicate the complexity of belief, even and simply from the perspective of the proposition itself. Whether will and intellect can be neatly distinguished is well beyond the scope of this study.

All these considerations of faith necessarily involve the individual. Faith presupposes consciousness. The relationship of belief, knowledge, and assent puzzled Augustine. Under the title "God Must First Be Known by an Unerring Faith, that He May Be Loved," Augustine asks "whether something can be loved which is unknown, because if it cannot then no one loves God before he knows Him" (*De trinitate* VIII.4.6, 247). We have encountered Augustine's position regarding the eternal God, that contemplation of such is wisdom, separate from the temporal world. Assuming that man cannot know the essence of God, and assuming further that one cannot love what one does not know, then there appears to be no way for man to love God. But Augustine notes "we must first love by faith, or it will be impossible for our hearts to be purified and become fit and worthy to see him ... So something can be loved which is unknown, provided it is believed" (*De trinitate* VIII.4.6, 247). Faith, according to Augustine, must provide enough knowledge, if not wisdom, in order to elicit love, which may be the assent that Aquinas requires for belief. Perhaps what faith provides is a thirst or desire that substitutes for knowledge, a craving so sublime that it persuades the individual without satisfying the desire.

I have asserted that the Incarnation is an affront to reason, that it is nonsense. Augustine claims that it "so offends the proud" (*De trinitate* XIII.17.22, 364). By my assertion I do not claim nor even mean to imply that the Incarnation is not or cannot be real. Various writers describe faith to be an elevation, even the perfection of reason (Aquinas). Thus it may be worthwhile to try to be more precise about the way in which the Incarnation, which is a symbol, article, or proposition of Christianity, does not make sense, the way in which it affronts or forms a conflict with reason.

Paul Tillich delineates four dimensions of truth, each largely or entirely separate from the other three. In addition to faith, the other dimensions are historical, scientific, and philosophical. Tillich claims, for example, that the truths of science cannot come into conflict with the truths of faith: "Science can conflict only with science, and faith only with faith" (*Dynamics of Faith* 95). If only that were the case! How can an individual, a living person who holds a tenet of faith or who "knows" a truth of science, not hear the other side beckoning? At one point, Tillich defines faith as "the state of being grasped by the power of being which transcends everything that is" (*Courage* 159) and, at another, following Luther, he claims: "Faith is the state of being ultimately concerned" (*Dynamics of Faith* 1). The state of faith is characterized by symbols, one of which is the Incarnation. The Incarnation is not an image of a birth, but rather an assertion or a proposition of a truth. One's ultimate concern may include this symbol, this truth. When phrased as a proposition, the symbol shares aspects with all four of Tillich's dimensions.

The Incarnation does not symbolize merely a general truth of faith, that God became man, but rather it symbolizes a particular event, the Son of God became the man Jesus of Nazareth, Jesus Christ. Thus the historical is involved. If our rich symbol includes the virgin birth, then the scientific, by being offended, comes into play. Most important, the philosophical is offended by the mixing of the eternal with the temporal, and thus it too is involved. Eternal action, changeless, humbled itself to become a creature and suffer time. "Just as he accepted slavery, so he accepted time" (Augustine, *Enarrationes* 74.5). Thus we have one hypostasis, one substance, Jesus Christ, eternal and temporal, changeless and changing, creator and created. We have Kierkegaard's paradox.

5

Faith and Works

The inherent contradiction between the mode of faith and the objective of faith results in anxiety. Love may be patient (1 Cor. 13:4), but faith is not, at least not to the extent that it can be conceived as an entity different from love. We saw that a promise of faith is eternal life, the beatific vision, but there is nothing eternal about faith. Faith is a part of life, a never-ending activity in pursuit of knowledge. The person of faith suffers time. With the attainment of knowledge comes the end of faith in two senses. First, knowledge, as the beatific vision, is the completion of faithfulness, according to Jesus (Jn 17:3). Second, as evidence accumulates for the thing desired, as certainty of things seen replaces "conviction of things not seen," the need for faith may diminish, depending upon the object. The knowledge sought in the first sense may be related to the second kind and thus be made up of empirical instances. Therefore, faith may be thought of as empirical, while being in itself universal, infinite, absolute. Faith is fundamentally existential. The anxiety arises from the conflict of knowledge with existing, with time. With regard to anxiety and existence, faith may be considered a special case. Human existence may imply anxiety, but that is a broader topic that is not pursued here.

One might think that the contradiction of faith arises only in the case of Jesus Christ, in the case where eternal significance is attributed to an historical event. This is Kierkegaard's position, and certainly much of the complexity and many of the difficulties associated with faith are uniquely manifested in the case of religious faith. I maintain, however, that the inherent contradiction extends to all forms of faith. It is true that, unlike the Son of God become man, neither gold, the nation, nor the beloved is eternal, the latter at least not in bodily form. But finitude and temporality do not obviate the contradiction between the mode of faith and its objective. The believer expects gold to hold its value endlessly. The same is true for the patriot and for the lover.

What does the person of faith do? Can he be identified by his actions? Kierkegaard would have us believe that such a person is indistinguishable from another person lacking faith (see the burgher in *Fear and Trembling* 39–40). But perhaps we should inquire further into the mode of faith. What does the person of faith do? He believes, i.e., he thinks or asserts something even if that assertion is merely trust. The person of faith declares it, in words and by his actions. Augustine and Aquinas would say he thinks it and then wills or assents to it. Then the person of faith waits, then declares again, then waits some more. He is waiting in pursuit. In short, he exists, but this declaring and waiting soon become unbearable. The person of faith is an anxious person, doubly anxious, and invariably this anxiety transforms itself into action. The person of faith acts. He performs deeds and obeys. Deeds, obedience, and public declarations are all forms of assent, or so the believer would like to think, and the declarations are intended to be convincing both inwardly and outwardly.

These steps or stages are listed here as if they occur sequentially in time. First the person of faith believes. Then he declares. Then he waits. Then he obeys. But this succession is not necessarily a temporal sequence. It is delineated so in an attempt to understand the relationship between faith and works.

Let us consider the works or actions themselves. They can be construed as evidence of faith, a manifestation of an inner disposition, an assent. Can works be more than evidence, can the works themselves constitute either an act of faith or the knowledge that faith pursues, or both? Can the believer give himself a sign of his faith? Does his public confession, his obedience, or his work constitute the assent that characterizes belief, according to Augustine and Aquinas?

With regard to faith in Jesus Christ, Paul's statements on the subject of faith and works are famous. From Galatians, we have "man is not justified by works of the law but through faith in Jesus Christ" (2:16). "If justification (δικαιοσύνη) were through the law then Christ died for no purpose" (Gal. 2:21). "Foolish Galatians … did you receive the Spirit by works of the law or by hearing from faith?" (Gal. 3:1-2). From Romans: "For if Abraham was justified by works, he has something to boast about, but not before God. Abraham believed (ἐπίστευσεν) God and it was reckoned (ἐλογίσθη) to him as righteousness" (4:2-3) (Paul is quoting Gen. 15:6). Paul clarifies his meaning of reckoned by drawing an analogy, in fact a distinction, between owing and reckoning: "Now to one who works, his wages are not reckoned as a gift but as his due. And to one who does not work but trusts him who justifies the ungodly, his faith is reckoned as righteousness" (Rom. 4:4-5).

In Colossians, however, Paul seems to indicate that good works are connected to knowledge of God:

> And so, from the day we heard of it, we have not ceased to pray for you, asking that you may be filled with the knowledge of his will in all spiritual wisdom and understanding, to lead a life worthy of the Lord, fully pleasing to him, bearing fruit in every good work and increasing in the knowledge [ἐπιγνώσει—full knowledge] of God. (Col. 1:9-10)

There are then the famous, perhaps infamous, remarks in the Letter of James that on the face of it seem to contradict Paul's separation of works from justification. "What does it profit, my brethren, if a man says he has faith but has not works? Can his faith save him?" (Jas 2:14). "So faith by itself, if it has not works, is dead" (Jas 2:17). "Was not Abraham our father justified by works, when he offered his son Isaac upon the altar?" (Jas 2:21).

Paul and James, then, appear to contradict one another. Martin Luther thought that the Letter of James did not belong to the biblical canon (*Preface to the Epistles of St. James and St. Jude*). This is so because Luther emphatically endorses the sentiments of Paul that I have just presented. With utter confidence, Luther asserts that the person of faith is justified by faith alone. He writes: "No one keeps the law by 'works'" (*Preface to Romans* 20). "Faith ... cannot do other than good at all times .... Hence, the man of faith, without being driven, willingly and gladly seeks to do good to everyone, serve everyone, suffer all kinds of hardships ... It is impossible ... to separate works from faith" (*Preface to Romans* 24). From Luther's *The Freedom of a Christian*, we have: "Hence a man [of faith] cannot be idle ... Nevertheless the works themselves do not justify him before God, but he does the works out of spontaneous love in obedience to God ... " (68) and "Good works do not make a good man, but a good man does good works" (69).

One of Luther's most bold and clarifying claims regarding faith and works occurs in *The Freedom of a Christian*, where he writes: "the First Commandment, which says, 'You shall worship one God,' is fulfilled by faith alone .... Works proceed from fulfillment of the commandments" (62). My interpretation of this remark, following Paul, is that no one can merely keep the commandments. Paul writes: "For all who rely on works of the law are under a curse; for it is written, 'Cursed be every one who does not abide by all things written in the book of the law, and do them'" (Gal. 3:10). The quotation is from Deuteronomy 27:26, but Paul has added "all things" (πᾶσιν). He confirms his conception of all or nothing, or perhaps I should say "all and nothing," two chapters later. "I testify again to every man who receives circumcision that he is bound to keep the whole law" (Gal. 5:3). Paul may have the authority of Jesus supporting him in this matter. During the feast of Tabernacles, Jesus taught in the temple: "Did not Moses give you the law. Yet none of you keeps the law" (Jn 7:19). And metaphorically: "No one who puts his hand to the plow and looks back is fit for the kingdom of God" (Lk. 9:62). Thus one must keep all the commandments perfectly, or one must follow completely the Lord Jesus Christ, leaving the dead to bury the dead.

It is common to see or read remarks regarding the difficulty or impossibility of keeping the Tenth Commandment regarding coveting. (It is noteworthy that both the First and Tenth Commandments address the interior man. Thus no action or inaction can unquestionably demonstrate obedience.) Luther's treatment, however, is that no one can keep even the First Commandment on his own. "I am the LORD your God ... You shall have no other gods before me" (Exod. 20:2-3; Deut. 5:6-7). Moses goes on to explain the meaning of this commandment. "Hear, O Israel: The LORD our God is one LORD; and you shall love the LORD your God with all your heart, and with all your soul, and with all your might" (Deut. 6:4-5). Jesus concurs. "Hear, O Israel: The LORD our God, the LORD is one; and you shall love the LORD your God with all your heart, and with all your soul, and with all your mind, and with all your strength" (Mk 12:29-30; Mt. 22:37; Lk. 10:27). No one who looks back.

According to Calvin, primitive man was able to keep this commandment because he was made in the image of God and thus his uncompromised reason ruled his actions (*Institutes* I.15, S.3, 107). But the disordered nature of fallen man is unable to love the Lord above all. Aquinas asserts that "in the state of corrupted nature man falls short of this in the appetite of his rational will, which unless it be cured by God's grace, follows its private good" (*Summa theologica* II.i, Q.109, A.3). Only by means of charity which comes by means of the grace of the Holy Spirit is fallen man able to love God above all, and this only momentarily (*Summa theologica* II.i, Q.108, A.1). In order to persevere in the state of total, dedicated love of God, man needs a continuous infusion of grace (*Summa theologica* II.i, Q.109, A.8–10).

Luther's understanding is similar, I believe, to that of Augustine at the pivotal moment of conversion that is related in his *Confessions* (VIII.xii.29). Augustine is called to take up and read from Paul's letter to the Romans: "Let us conduct ourselves becomingly as in the day, not in reveling and drunkenness ... But put on the Lord Jesus Christ, and make no provision for the flesh, to gratify its desires" (13:13-14). In his letters to the Galatians (3:27), Ephesians (4:22-4), and Colossians (3:9-10), Paul also expresses the need to put on (ἐνδύω) a new self. One must repudiate the flesh (σάρξ), which for Paul signifies all of human nature, not just lust or physical desire. He provides more details when distinguishing between the works of the spirit and the works of the flesh. "Now the works of the flesh are plain: fornication, impurity, licentiousness, idolatry, sorcery, enmity, strife, jealousy, anger, selfishness, dissention, party spirit (αἵρεσις), envy, drunkenness, carousing, and the like" (Gal. 5:19-21). The central theme of Paul's letters is that the individual cannot abide by the law. The individual cannot save himself through scrupulous effort to perform certain actions and to refrain from performing other, sinful acts. Only by putting on the Lord Jesus Christ, in giving oneself over to him, can one hope for salvation and to be justified.

In addition to the Apostle Paul, Augustine is a source for this way of thinking, especially of Luther and Calvin. In his anti-Pelagian treatises, Augustine argues at length that man is saved by grace alone and that works contain no salvific merit. (These treatises are remarkable for their didactic nature and unrelenting stance, in contrast to the questioning character of many of Augustine's other works.)

The predominant, even overwhelming, opinion of the theologians just cited is that justification comes about from faith in God, and here particularly in Jesus of Nazareth as the Christ. Paul, Augustine, Luther, and Calvin seem to be univocal in this opinion, and many writers have subsequently followed them. But not all. First of all, there is the letter of James which emphasizes works and provides the foundation for "dead faith." There are remarks by Paul, also, that do not seem to accord entirely with this idea of justification. On judgment day, God "will render to every man according to his works," eternal life or wrath and fury (Rom. 2:6-8). Karl Barth attempts to accommodate this dissonance by asserting, if works do in fact have some merit, that merit is determined solely by God (*Epistle* 432).

Buber would identify Luther's position as an extension of the Hellenic repositioning by Paul of Judaism and the teachings of Jesus. For Buber, God is satisfied with man who trusts in him according to his nature (*Two Types of Faith* 79–80). God is not a law-giver but a teacher (*Two Types of Faith* 56-7). Thereby, Paul, Augustine, Luther, and Calvin become impractical, extremist zealots.

The First Commandment requires that only the God of Abraham, a person-God, be adored. As indicated in Chapter 3, we all worship at the temples of several gods. Even among devout Christians such as Augustine, polytheistic behavior occurs: "Each man, no matter how praiseworthy his life may be, succumbs now and then to bodily lusts" (*City of God* I.9). Monotheism is practically impossible. Paul, Augustine, and Luther acknowledge the universal failure to keep the First Commandment, and recommend in its stead a relinquishment that amounts to faith in Jesus Christ, i.e., in believing that Jesus of Nazareth is the Christ, the Son of God. "Put on the Lord Jesus Christ, and make no provision ... " (Rom. 13:14).

Here I attempt to emphasize this acknowledgment by claiming that no one can keep the law perfectly. I claim that no one can keep the faith perfectly. In Romans (2:17-24), Paul accuses the Jews of being inward hypocrites with respect to the law. I assert something that everyone already knows, that all the faithful are hypocrites.

Idolatry, strictly speaking, refers to the adoration of man-made objects in lieu of the proper object of faith and adoration. The Second Commandment forbids this activity. "You shall not make for yourself a graven image, or any likeness of anything that is in heaven above, ... you shall not bow down to them or serve them" (Exod. 20:4-6; Deut. 5:8-10). If Barth is correct in his claim that "there is no theological visual art," then we might be unable to violate the first part of this commandment ("Humanity of God" 57). But the problem of idolatry is much broader than images of things that are in heaven. Paul and other Christian writers expand the definition to include worship of anything other than the proper object of worship. The expansion and generalization are especially clear in Colossians, where Paul writes: "Put to death therefore what is earthly in you: fornication, impurity, passion, evil desire, and covetousness, which is idolatry" (3:5; see also Eph. 5:5). And in Galatians: "For the desires of the flesh are against the Spirit, and the desires of the Spirit are against the flesh" (5:17-21; see also 1 Cor. 8:1-13; 10:6-8; 10:14; 12:1-2). It takes little effort to propose candidates for idolatrous worship: country, family, church. Should reason and life also be placed on this list? Pope Francis warns that idolatry consists of disintegration or disunity wherein the fundamental orientation of our existence "breaks down into the multiplicity of [our] desires" (*Lumen fidei* I.13). How can one help but break down into a multiplicity of desires? Can it possibly be that our every inclination that deviates from worship of the one God, the person-God, is idolatrous?

Idolatry now includes multiple gods, as if the physical representation of a god had been promoted to the level of genuine substitute, an alternative god. Accordingly, the Second Commandment becomes subsumed under the First. We can add Jesus to the list of extremists, at least with regard to some of his remarks. "You have heard that it was said, 'You shall not commit adultery.' But I say to you that every one who looks at a woman lustfully has already committed adultery with her in his heart" (Mt. 5:27-8).

We worship at many temples. The First Commandment, or its equivalent for faiths in other gods, cannot be kept by force of human will. Paul, drawing from Psalm 14:3, writes: "None is righteous, no, not one" (Rom. 3:10). "All have sinned and fall short of the glory of God" (Rom. 3:23). We are all idolaters. And must we extend this severe interpretation to all forms of faith? Is not each and every spouse guilty of infidelity? The lovers who have sanctified that love through marriage then proceed to live the rest of their lives in idolatrous betrayal.

It should be noted that Bonhoeffer, in his late writings, recoils at this expanded understanding of idolatry. He asserts that the expanded list of idols is unbiblical. But his criticism is founded more on a contemporary and prevailing lack of reverence for anything (*Letters from Prison* 336). This apparent change in Bonhoeffer's thinking from his earlier *The Cost of Discipleship* results from his interpretation of the First Commandment, an interpretation quite different from the one proposed by Luther and adopted here, an interpretation more in accord with Buber's understanding. According to Bonhoeffer, "earthly affection" forms a counterpoint to our eternal, whole-hearted love of God. Presumably this counterpoint is euphonious (*Letters from Prison* 303). Support for this line of thinking might be found in the First Letter of John. "For this is the love of God, that we keep his commandments. And his commandments are not burdensome" (1 Jn 5:3). Are God's commandments not burdensome?

Many authors follow Luther and expand his claims regarding faith and works. Barth becomes antagonistic in his rejection of the power of works: "A Francis of Assisi is condemned by the Truth by which a Caesar Borgia is set free" (*Epistle* 288). "Works bring men into relationship with a god whom they can comprehend, not the God who doeth miracles" (*Epistle* 367). "There are no moral actions such as love, or honesty, or purity, or courage, which have rid themselves of the *form of this world*, which are not 'erotic'" (*Epistle* 434).

What is the believer to do? One can seek the support of like-minded believers, what is often called religious fellowship. Although such association may be helpful, it seems to be so only in a mundane and temporal way. Like-minded friends and associates can help to put off, to postpone confronting the conflict between the objective of faith, knowledge, and the mode of faith, existing, waiting, acting, suffering, and obeying. Even the zealot Paul acknowledges the benefit of fellowship in writing to the Romans (1:11-12). But religious fellowship, mutual encouragement does not eliminate the conflict. Apparently it attempts to assuage an eternal problem with temporal balm. Sooner or later the remedy will wear off, and the believer will become the idle believer, the lonely sinner.

We have seen that faith that is not preoccupied with works seeks its own undoing. It seeks to be annihilated by knowledge of the object. Faith is not settled; it is not settling, but rather unsettling. One does not repose in faith, one struggles. I assert this in rebuke to those who would criticize the faithful as complacent, as sheep. I acknowledge, however, that the critics at times seem to interpret correctly the assertions of the "defenders of the faith." I ask again, what is the believer to do?

Mindful that I still have not delved into the cause of this instability, I offer the following answer. Works. Actions. According to Bonhoeffer, faith, not obedience, justifies, but they are inseparable chronologically. By obedience Bonhoeffer means something akin to works and actions. He states further: "There is no faith without good works and no good works apart from faith" (*Discipleship* 295). Aquinas had developed notions of formed and unformed faith. He claims that charity quickens the act of faith, thereby forming it (*Summa theologica* II.ii, Q.4, A.3–4). Aquinas cites the famous line from the Letter of James as evidence of formless faith: "So faith by itself, if it has not works, is dead" (Jas 2:17). Aquinas maintains that formed and unformed faith are the same habit, pertaining to the intellect. The will is distinct from the thinking portion of the intellect, and charity pertains to the will (*Summa theologica* II.ii, Q.4, A.4). Further scriptural evidence can be found in Paul's writings. "For in Christ Jesus neither circumcision nor uncircumcision is of any avail, but faith working through love" (Gal. 5:6). Bonhoeffer and others have, in effect, swept away this distinction between formed and unformed faith, determining it to be meaningless.

By analogy, one might think of a physicist who claims that space-time is the real context of the material world. In mathematical thinking, one can analyze space-time into its apparent constituent parts, space and time, but these are separable parts only in thought. In this world space-time is what matters. Thus, according to Bonhoeffer, although justification comes through faith alone, not through works, the two are not separable in time. They are separable only in reasoning about justification. The believer acts. Why?

6

Faith and Time, or Choking on Faith

Works are the anxiety of faith, the realization and playing out of faith's temporality. These days, it seems as though everyone suffers from anxiety (*anxiety*, from Greek ἄγχω and Latin *angere, to strangle, throttle, choke*). For the past century it has been claimed that we live in an age of anxiety. It is not my intent to speculate about this claim. The person of faith at any time lives an anxious life, suffers from anxiety, chokes. This is not a historical argument. One may fear the wrath of God, which is the demand of justice that the wicked be punished; but one is anxious in faith, in seeking that which, as long as one exists, cannot be obtained.

The meaning of anxiety in our lives is much broader than our consideration. Kierkegaard understands anxiety in and as time, existence, possibility, sin, and despair (*Concept of Anxiety*). Heidegger, too, acknowledges anxiety as a necessary state of mind, of *Dasein* (*Being and Time* H266). Following these authors, Paul Tillich even provides a taxonomy of anxiety founded on the individual's awareness of nonbeing, Heidegger's "Being-towards-death" (*Courage* 34). He proposes a historical unfolding of anxiety, with various periods identified with particular manifestations of anxiety.

I do not deny that time and place shape our thought, and, along with Don Quixote, I suspect that we live in an Age of Iron. Nor do I deny the ever-present dichotomy of collectivism and individuality. At certain times and places our thinking may give more evidence of one side of the dichotomy than the other. But the anxiety of faith in general is intrinsic to faith in general. It may manifest itself in somewhat different ways throughout history. This anxiety is not ahistorical but rather all-historical, participating in the fullness of time. My treatment of anxiety, however, is limited and peculiar to faith. I am not speaking about the broader notion of anxiety as a manifestation of sin.

How does anxiety arise and how do works come forth? One might seek clarification between faith and works and especially in how works issue from faith in comments made by Jesus after he has multiplied the loaves and fishes to feed the crowd. Jesus admonished his listeners to seek not food that perishes but rather the food of eternal life. "Then they said to him, 'What must we do, to be doing the works of God?' Jesus answered them, 'This is the work of God, that you believe in him whom he has sent'" (Jn 6:28-9).

The people have asked Jesus, what are the works of God, what must one do in order to be a minister of God? According to Jesus, the work of God is belief in the one whom God has sent, Jesus Christ. Knowledge of "him whom [God] has sent" is the essential part of the completion of faith, which is eternal life (Jn 17:3). But the people have asked here for guidance in living a faithful life, guidance regarding the conduct of a person of faith. They are not inquiring into the end of faith but rather about faith's method and activity. According to Jesus, belief in him is the modus operandi for obtaining the end of faith, knowledge of him. His remarks do not fit neatly with those of Luther and Calvin who would have us believe that works issue forth from faith. Jesus seems to indicate that faith, or more precisely belief, *is* the work.

Faith, inherently temporal, entails belief. Aquinas separates belief into two activities, one of the knowing intellect and one of the will. Applying this understanding to the passage from John, we obtain the following. Belief or the act of faith constitutes assent to the proposition "Jesus is the Christ, the one whom God has sent." Although Jesus characterizes belief as a work here, this does not resolve the matter of whether or not there are both formed and unformed faith, one living and one dead. Luther, Bonhoeffer et al. understand works as issuing forth immediately from faith. One cannot separate faith from works and, by extension, one cannot separate belief from works. In their minds, thinking that "Jesus is the Christ, the one whom God has sent" is neither belief nor a proposition of faith. It is indeed a proposition in a grammatical sense: this is that. It is an article of faith only in this syntactical or grammatical sense. As a genuine article of faith, it is an expression of belief and, as such, in the words of Jesus, it is a work of God performed by men; it is an act of faith.

Works result from the contradiction of the mode of faith and the intent of faith. They are evidence of the doubt and struggle that Calvin speaks of, such "that the minds of believers are seldom at rest" (*Institutes* III.2, S.17, 366–7; S.37, 379). Works are signs that point to the object of faith without necessarily advancing the objective of faith. One might wish for works to play a more constructive role in faith's pursuit, and might even claim that they do. Why cannot they serve similarly as evidence of faithfulness by the object of faith? For Abraham to believe it was necessary although insufficient that there be signs of the LORD's faithfulness: e.g., Isaac. Conversely, works may serve as necessary although insufficient signs of fidelity on the part of the believer. But if they so serve, it is difficult to see how their temporal, particular, and finite nature would accumulate sufficiently to make an advance on an eternal and infinite goal.

Here is the problem that any person of faith of any kind faces. He would like to be certain about the object of faith. He would like to know it, to move beyond "assurance of things hoped for, conviction of things not seen" to certain knowledge. He would also like to be certain about his own faithfulness. Thus there are two sides to the faith relation. One might think that all the difficulty resides on one side, on that of the object of faith. Is God? How is He? Does He care for us? These concerns are common to any person of faith and with some modification to any object of faith: a lover, a country, Dulcinea, the world, one's own common sense.

Upon further inquiry, however, one realizes that the difficulty, the uncertainty, also resides on the other side, on the side of self-knowledge. We may tell ourselves that our intent is pure, our trustworthiness is certain, and our care for and concern about the object unquestionable. But such assertions are simply and clearly false, and we know it. In fact, our self-knowledge is perhaps greater than we would like in this matter, because we know that our intent is mitigated, our trustworthiness questionable, and our care and concern fluctuating and sporadic.

Can you give yourself a sign? Is not faith simply and strictly a gift. Countless authors describe it as such. Thus, can you willingly perform an action or obey a command that would serve as evidence of faith? To the extent that the work or obedience is such evidence, then the answer is "yes," but immediately one wants to ask another question: "Why would anyone want to perform a work?" Perhaps some examples of works may help.

Switching all of your savings from US dollars into gold would constitute an act of faith in the gold-god. Ignoring lipstick on your lover's collar, or its equivalent, while doing the laundry might be another such act: simply apply the stain remover and put the shirt into the washing machine. Trusting your own reason and common sense, although they are contradicted by a knowledgeable authority such as your government or your mother, would seem to be evidence of faith. Fasting, not eating pork, and going to church on Sundays would also be signs.

By "give yourself a sign," however, I first want to know if you can persuade yourself that gold will preserve its value, that your lover is faithful to you, that your mother is wrong, that there is a God, i.e., give a sign that is truly meaningful and significant, a trustworthy sign. No, of course not. Complete persuasion is not an aspect of faith. Indeed, complete persuasion is the annihilation of faith, its transformation from faith into knowledge. Complete persuasion is contained in the beatific vision, although presumably the beatific vision is richer than mere certainty. But maybe not, for certainly we have no experience of complete certainty other than of our own self-awareness. Perhaps we might think of the beatific vision as total certainty about everything. Let us keep in mind also that persuasion is different from forgetting or growing too tired to care. For example, fatigue plays a role in Don Quixote's apostasy near the end of his life. Fatigue seems to be a terribly uninteresting cause of infidelity. Such an explanation amounts to claiming that the person of faith simply lost interest in the object of faith. But if we interpret fatigue to be the inexorable suffering under time, then it becomes intrinsic to the life of faith.

Let me consider a less lofty goal. Not knowledge, not persuasion, not even the "assurance of things hoped for." Can an individual, by acting, will evidence of his own faith into existence? What I want to consider is the opposite of the famous remark of James about faith without works. In brief, can there be a work without faith?

In a limited sense, the answer is "yes." If we consider the performance of some act, e.g., the removal of a lipstick stain from a shirt collar, without considering the intention behind the act, then surely there is no evidence of faith in a lover. If the intent is simply and strictly to launder the shirt, then again there is no evidence of faith. If one attends church on Sunday because one enjoys the music, this act is evidence of faith, but not faith in the person-God. These are not the faithless acts that interest me. I want to know if one can will a sign of his own faith, his own trustworthiness, for which one must know the answer to a prior or deeper question. Why would one want to give himself a sign? Could not the desire to provide such a sign for oneself be an indication, albeit psychological, of a mustard seed of faith, a mustard seed of desire, by which I mean merely an inkling of the desire to pursue the knowledge? A haunting?

We must beware here of a subtle kind of hypocrisy. In Romans, Paul seems at one point to be calling the Jews hypocrites (2:17-24): "But if you call yourself a Jew and rely upon the law and boast of your relation to God ... you then who teach others, will you not teach yourself? While you preach against stealing, do you steal? You who say that one must not commit adultery, do you commit adultery? ... " and so forth. Luther observes that the hypocrisy does not consist in commanding others not to steal while being in fact a thief. He asserts that Paul acknowledges that his audience abides by the law in the sense of performing certain required actions while abstaining from other prohibited actions. But Paul, according to Luther, charges his audience with observing a law that is hated. The observant hypocrites fear punishment or hope for recompense, but they do not obey the law out of love for God (Luther, *Preface to Romans* 20). For Luther, this fear of the law is not respect and awe but rather fear of the consequence of breaking the law. This is the fear of the hypocrite, who is not blessed, who admonishes the adulterer while desiring to perform the same act. Thus one must proceed cautiously when inquiring about works.

In Chapter 4 we considered the claim by Augustine and Aquinas that *to believe* is to think with assent. I now ask whether works might constitute such assent. Luther claims that faith and works are inseparable. Bonhoeffer makes the analogous claim that one does not believe today and then begin to obey tomorrow (*Discipleship* 63–4). "Only he who believes is obedient ... [and] only he who is obedient believes" ("Cost of Discipleship" 172). Works are the outward signs of faith, or more properly, the signs. How reliable are these signs?

Aquinas identifies an unformed faith, faith without charity (*Summa theologica* II.ii, Q.4, A.3–4). Presumably such a faith might entail public or outward confessions of the articles of faith, but this kind of faith would lack the charitable disposition and actions that are indicative of formed faith. On this account, assent may be identified with an action: works and obedience. Faith is thus perfected by charity. One could, of course, perform actions that have the appearance of charitable works but are in fact motivated by something other than charity. One might attempt to appear generous out of vain self-interest. We have seen that Bonhoeffer and others reject the distinction between formed and unformed faith.

For our purposes, however, even if we accept the distinction, we must evaluate the assent to see what effect it has on the anxiety that accompanies faith. The assent itself is a visible or audible act, a public confession, an act of obedience, or an act of charity. Under Luther's interpretation, we ask if the act is motivated by faith. Under Aquinas's interpretation, we ask if the act is motivated by charity. In either case, the interior act or disposition determines the true character of the outward sign. Can we know our interior acts?

Luther notes that the true Christian gives himself "as a Christ" to one's neighbor (*Freedom of a Christian* 75). This person of faith does not live for self, but "lives also for all men on earth" (*Freedom of a Christian* 73). The true believer seeks to "serve and benefit others in all that he does, considering nothing except the need and the advantage of his neighbor" (*Freedom of a Christian* 73). This person of faith has charity, and one might wonder if this blessed state could in some way alleviate the anxiety that attends faith, the anxiety that results in "faithful" action. I presume that a person in this state is the Christian who is truly free. But no one can know the certainty of one's faith. Certitude is the end of faith. There may be true Christians among us. I presume that, if they are here, they would also be among those who doubt their faith.

Thus the question regarding interior acts amounts to a rephrasing of the initial inquiry concerning signs: can you give yourself a sign? To do so with certainty would require that we truly know our disposition, that we clearly distinguish between inclination and will, that we determine the freedom of our action, that we know ourselves. But the freedom of our actions as well as those of others remains a mystery to us despite our ardent desire for certain actions to be free. Kant extends this claim necessarily to include our own morality in general. We may perform certain acts that are deemed generally to be moral and virtuous, but do we perform them in true freedom? A person donates to the poor. We describe the act as generous and charitable. We assign merit to the person. But do we really know the person's character? Can we see clearly into his soul? What if the person in question has, in Kant's words, a "fortunate (*glücklich*) constitution. And hence no one can pass judgment in accordance with complete justice" (*Critique of Pure Reason* A551/B579, n. 339). Alas, we are equally ignorant about our own constitution, and accordingly cannot know with certainty our own virtue or vice. If we adopt this position, we encounter the following difficulty with faith as delineated by Aquinas. Faith entails belief. To believe is to think with assent. Our very own assent is open to doubt. At best, we might say, the person of faith can only believe that he believes. Such a person is anxious. Certainly, this conclusion regarding works and anxiety could have been anticipated. One who, along with Kierkegaard, understood the relationship between anxiety and sin might have come to the same conclusion. For only sinners are faithful.

Works are the anxiety of faith, which is an inherently contradictory activity, an action or effort to accumulate piecemeal an infinite quantity in a finite amount of time. Some authors, especially Kierkegaard, see the anxiety as a result of existence. But existence may be too broad or general a term, conflating or stitching together being with time. It is the temporality of existence, time, that conflicts with the objective of faith, knowledge. The person of faith wants to know an eternal truth about temporal matters. He would like to understand something like the Incarnation, but to comprehend it he must wait, apparently. If I am correct about succession and logical entailment, he may be able to know an eternal or necessary truth, but only momentarily, although perhaps repeatedly momentarily. He must suffer time in hope and anticipation of participation in the timeless, but participation not at some future time. One might unsympathetically view this kind of thinking as a desire to be through with it all, to be relieved of hellish waiting.

Because faith is temporal, the person of faith is always on trial. This state of the condition or passion is indicated by two words at the end of the temptation of Jesus as reported by Luke. The biblical passage is famous in which Jesus, fasting in the wilderness, is tempted by the devil (Mt. 4:1-11; Lk. 4:1-13). Jesus' reply to the third temptation differs in the two accounts, but what follows is of greater importance here. The passage in Matthew concludes (4:11): Then the devil left him, and behold, angels came and ministered to him. Luke concludes (4:13): And when the devil had ended every temptation, he departed from him for a time (ἄχρι καιροῦ). The final two words in Luke's version indicate that the temptation of Jesus has ended only for a while. In this passage, Jesus demonstrates his faithfulness to God in the face of the three-fold assault of the devil. In Matthew's version, Jesus, having resisted the temptation, is ministered to by angels. In Luke's version the assault ends, but the final two words indicate ominously that there will be further assaults in the future. How can there not be! Faith, which is always temporal, is never finished. Faith *is* trial. By his act of faith, the person of faith does not abolish temptation. Abraham must ascend Mount Moriah again, each morning.

One might think, even hope, that the kind or type of faith that Martin Buber identifies with pre-Hellenic Israel would be free from this anxiety. According to Buber, instead of the Pauline notion of "all or nothing," ancient Judaism demands a kind of adherence that is suited to mankind. "God expects from thee fulfilment according to thy nature and ability ... not less, but also not more" (*Two Types of Faith* 79–80). The Torah is not the law but rather a guide. God is not a law-giver but a teacher (*Two Types of Faith* 56–7). Buber maintains that even Jesus had this conception of faith.

Such a conception of faith is epitomized in the Aaronic benediction. "The LORD bless you and keep you: The LORD make his face to shine upon you, and be gracious to you" (Num. 6:22-7). Faith becomes trust in the LORD that He "make his face to shine upon" us. But the Bible is full of pleading with the LORD. "Do not hide thy face from me in the day of my distress!" (Ps. 102:2). "Restore us, O God; let thy face shine, that we may be saved!" (Ps. 80:3, 7, 19). "My soul thirsts for God, for the living God. When shall I come and behold the face of God" (Ps. 42:2). These pleas exhibit the anxiety that attends trust in someone.

For Heidegger, the anxiety is not peculiar to the person of faith because *Dasein* is futural (*als zukünftiges; Being and Time* H325), always on its way, with constantly something still to be settled (*Being and Time* H325, 79, 266). Granting these conditions as well as those regarding the revelation of the beatific vision, it would seem that the person of faith is especially and exceedingly in the throes of anxiety, double anxiety: the anxiety of life itself and the anxiety of the contradiction of faith.

Waiting is the test of time. Waiting in line, waiting at the doctor's office, waiting on hold. For much of life, time resides in the background, or perhaps as a penumbra surrounding our action. One needs to think about time. In play, time all but disappears only to intrude at the end of play, but in waiting we suffer time. Time steps forward. Waiting stands at the heart of faith. How hard is it to wait? Kierkegaard places himself in Abraham's shoes, having received the command from the LORD to sacrifice his beloved son Isaac. He writes that he would not have dawdled. "I am quite sure that I would have been punctual and all prepared—more than likely, I would have arrived too early in order to get it over sooner" (*Fear and Trembling* 34–5). Kierkegaard could not stand to wait to sacrifice his son.

In one respect, Barth turns the tables when it comes to waiting, asserting that it is God who waits for us. In his treatment of Paul's letter to the Romans, he translates πίστις as "the faithfulness of God" (*Epistle* 13–14). "Great is thy faithfulness" (Lam. 3:23). But the faithfulness attributed to God by Barth is a mirror of our faithfulness, no matter how imperfect our faithfulness may be. For the faithful person waits, but surely God does not wait. Thus God's waiting is a reflection of our own waiting, an imposition by us on God, which we call faithfulness. Faithfulness is an aspect of faith but not identical to it.

We wait in time for that which cannot occur in time. In Samuel Beckett's famous play about waiting, *Waiting for Godot*, Lucky embarks upon a tirade at the beginning where he refers to "a personal God ... outside time without extension," but he concludes that "time will tell" (28b). It will not. And yet we expect a resolution in time.

Paul proclaims that the waiting culminates in salvation, when he writes: "So with us; when we were children, we were slaves to the elemental spirits of the universe. But when the fullness of time had come, God sent forth his Son, born of woman, born under the law, to redeem those who were under the law, so that we might receive adoption as sons" (Gal. 4:3-5). Like the person of faith who desires to understand the Incarnation, Paul offers the poetic expression "fullness of time" to locate the occurrence of the creator become creature.

Recall that part of the definition of eternal life given by Jesus is knowledge of "Jesus Christ whom [God] has sent" (Jn 17:3). Just as the Incarnation occurred in the fullness of time, we might wonder if the knowledge of eternal life, the objective of faith, will occur in the fullness of time. Recall also Martha's expression regarding the Son of God, "he who is coming into the world" (Jn 11:27). In our wonder, we must keep in mind that the end of time is not in the future, nor is the beginning of time in the past. Time then becomes a mystery, one that greatly intrigued Augustine in the latter portion of his *Confessions*, and that intrigues us all.

As mysterious as it may be in itself, for us time is also a passion. Time happens, by which I mean that we encounter time as an alien, no matter how much or to what extent time also may be an inward condition. We sinners suffer time. Without eternity, timelessness, we are condemned to a life of faith, a life of waiting. But what, then, is faith, a pursuit of the temporal? We have a grasp of the eternal, or so it seems, in our understanding of the logical. We need not be faithless. We need not harden our hearts. We understand that the side and diagonal of a square are incommensurable. We distinguish equal from unequal. But we repeatedly confuse the temporal and the eternal. That is why we pray for Judas.

We interject time into timelessness, into eternity. Like atheism, we call the timeless by that which we claim it is not, time. With Judas we do not accept eternal despair. We are tempted by the temporal, by freedom, the ethical, and we succumb to temptation by offering a prayer for the repose of the soul of Judas. Heidegger, while acknowledging the interjection, would not agree with my characterization of it as temptation. To the contrary, for him the temptation comes from the opposite side, from the eternal. "It has long been known that ancient ontology works with 'Thing-concepts' and that there is a danger of 'reifying consciousness' ... *Why* does this reifying (*Verdinglichung*) always keep coming back to exercise its dominion?" (*Being and Time* H437).

We are tempted away from faith, from principle, from the object of faith, be that object the gold-god, the reason-god, the person-God. Here I am concerned with the particular temptation of time. Does the soul of Judas exist in time, is it in time? If so, perhaps it might repent. When we think of his soul, we consider his person, and in considering his person we cannot remove, do not know how to remove, time. When we pray for Judas, we pray for his temporal soul. In the *Brothers Karamazov* by Dostoevsky we learn that the Elder Zosima prays for the suicides, although such prayer is forbidden by the church (II.vi, 3[i], 323). We as readers approve of such prayer, and in doing so we join Zosima in injecting time into the eternal. Stupidly, we mimic the Incarnation in reverse.

It may seem that much of this chapter amounts to a psychological account of the anxiety that necessarily attends faith and the result of that anxiety, works. This may be so in those cases that concern faith in an object such as country, reason, or the world. The human psyche necessarily chokes on the aim of faith—knowledge—which is unattainable while the human being in pursuit is relentlessly attacked and put on trial. Thus the person of faith, under psychological pressure, acts. I maintain, however, that the account here is also theological, at least with respect to the person-God, for in this case the account concerns the relationship of the creature to his creator. It concerns the creature within all creation, who must attempt to make sense out of creation. The creature faces not only psychological pressure but also sin. The person of faith confronts the contradiction between his methods and the aim or end of those methods. The person of faith waits, choking on the sinfulness of time, and demands from himself an account for such a predicament. While acting, this person looks to God. A psychological explanation is insufficient for the person of faith.

I summarize the last two sections thus. Works will issue forth if there is anxiety, and faith is inherently and peculiarly anxious because it is inherently temporal. Faith is in the domain of sin. Faith is the temporal pursuit of knowledge, the truth. We choke on faith. There will be anxiety if there is time, if time is. Without time, faith is meaningless. Therefore, works are entailed by faith.

Works issue forth from faith. About this much, nearly all writers on the subject seem to agree. How the works arise, how the mechanism of faith works is another matter. Aquinas, in his account of what it means *to believe*, claims that the two faculties of intellect and will operate on the gift of faith. Tillich also sees love as the manifestation, the works of faith (*Dynamics of Faith* 116, 133–4). The person of faith is separated from the object of faith, which he desires, which he loves. Thus he acts.

In the treatment of *to believe*, in Chapter 4, we saw the difficulty in keeping separate the intellect and the will. If I go no further than Aquinas and Tillich, then I must say that what one person calls "love" I call "anxiety." In my analysis of faith, I identify the desire that accompanies Tillich's separation. It is the desire to know the object of faith. In an attempt to extend this account, I note the separation between the eternal and the temporal. Thus the works that accompany faith arise from the juxtaposition of the eternal with the temporal.

It may seem surprising that faith as described here could also be thought of as a gift or a passion. Faith has been depicted as a pursuit of knowledge. Shall such a condition or cause be thought of as a gift? Both gift and passion indicate passivity on the part of the faithful person. ("Condition" and "predicate" similarly imply an occurrence or a suffering by the person or substance.) Thus we must think about how someone to whom something happens can be a pursuer.

For the moment, let us call the object of faith the god. The recipient of the gift, the one who will in fact embark upon pursuit, is grabbed by the god, haunted. This god might be reason, country, or Dulcinea. In each case, the recipient is not passive in a temporal sense. Indeed, the person of faith, although he suffers in proportion to the extent that he is faithful, actively pursues the god. But the faithful person is the one who is grabbed and attempts to grab back. The mysterious appearance of the condition of faith may be indicated by wonder, care, or anxiety. It is likely that the one haunted by the god will experience all of these: wonder, care, and anxiety. Thus faith as a gift is like being blessed with a child.

What of faith in Jesus Christ? What if he is the truth? He is in time. He is eternal. Thus he is transcendent. Is he not the ideal object of faith, the one to whom we should be faithful, if he is who he is claimed to be?

CODE OF CONDUCT

Does faith also entail particular works, a code of conduct? I wish to distinguish this question from an inquiry into religious codes, customs of fellowship, and organizational bylaws. One might devise the latter on the basis of an understanding of the action demanded by faith. But codes, customs, and bylaws are also rooted in society, in all social organizations, and hence are separate from the concern here.

Faithful action must not be hypocritical, either externally or internally. The lover who cheats on the beloved acts in a way contrary to his espoused faith, as does the investor who hedges his exposure to gold while singing its praises as a store of value. As Luther has pointed out, the one who follows the law all the while hating it is also a hypocrite.

It seems hardly worth mentioning that the actions of a person of faith may not coincide exactly with prevailing customs and laws. Nonetheless, one is constantly looking to such a person and his actions in search of evidence for the goodness of his faith. Hence the uproar when the faithful person violates ethical codes. These violations range from the moderately impolite (preaching the name of Jesus Christ in the school yard) to the murderous.

An act of faith abhorrent to modern sensibility is human sacrifice, especially the sacrifice of children. This practice stands at the center of the trial of Abraham (Gen. 22). Subsequently we learn that the God of Israel opposed this practice. "And the LORD said to Moses, ... you shall not do as they do in the land of Canaan, to which I am bringing you" (Lev. 18:1-3). Ahaz, king of the Ammonites, who reigned in Jerusalem, "burned his sons as an offering, according to the abominable practices of the nations whom the LORD drove out before the people of Israel" (2 Chron. 28:1-3).

This practice is positive. A possession of great value, a child, is offered up to God. The conduct of Ahaz was evidence, an external sign of his faith. A similar passive practice persists to the present. Some cultures in Ethiopia, Madagascar, and elsewhere understand the birth of twins to be an ill omen, multiple births being characteristic of animals, not human beings. Accordingly, the twins are sometimes abandoned by the parents and left to die. (One of the most astonishing claims of Christian doctrine consists of the appropriation and transformation of the sacrifice to Moloch. Out of love for mankind, God offered up his first born, his son, to be "burned" in expiation for the sins of man. "For God so loved the world that he gave his only Son" [Jn 3:16-17].)

The Apostle Paul provides ample counsel regarding the conduct that should characterize the Christian. This code is distinct from rituals followed by the early church, although Paul also advises followers to adhere to these rituals. "I wrote to you not to associate with any one who bears the name of bother if he is guilty of immorality or greed, or is an idolater, reviler, drunkard, or robber"

(1 Cor. 5:11). Paul tells the disciples to decide matters of dispute among themselves rather than bringing one another into court (1 Cor. 6:1-8). He warns that "neither the immoral, nor idolaters, nor adulterers, nor sexual perverts, nor thieves, nor the greedy, nor drunkards, nor revilers, nor robbers will inherit the kingdom of God" (1 Cor. 6:9-10). He provides counsel regarding marriage (1 Cor. 7:1-16), and regarding speaking in tongues (1 Cor. 14:1-40).

The Christian is expected: to love one another; to never flag in zeal; to be patient in tribulation; to contribute to the needs of the saints, i.e., the church in Jerusalem; to bless those who persecute you; to associate with the lowly; to live peaceably with all; and never to avenge yourselves (Rom. 12:9-19). Thus it is clear that in Paul's mind there exists a detailed and specific code of conduct that will give evidence of discipleship. Such a code may in fact be highly desirable, albeit manifestly worldly, for a community that has been freed from adherence to strictures of the law. Ultimately, a code of conduct seeks to foster worldly signs of faithfulness. These signs, such as circumcision, are for all, both fellow believers and non-believers. Are they signs of faith?

7

The Individual

The individual is significant for anxious faith in two respects, first as an individual, a person of faith in some god. The second respect concerns the peculiar kind of knowledge that is promised by Jesus in his definition of eternal life, not only of "thee the only true God" but also of the individual Jesus Christ "whom thou hast sent." With the person of faith one must distinguish between gods that are conceived as persons, e.g., Dulcinea or the person-God, and other gods such as reason or gold, but in either case one side of the relationship, the individual's, is held by a person. We are dealing with an individual who has a notion of self, who possesses consciousness and conscience. To give an account of these aspects of the individual lies well beyond the scope of my study.

I must address, however, the aspects of self-respect, self-love, and responsibility that attend the human being. It is commonly observed that dogs are faithful and trustworthy. They enter into faith relationships, and they seem to be capable of feeling shame. They trust that their masters have their well-being as a concern. In turn, dogs seem to have genuine interest in the well-being of their masters. Whether or not dogs are in need of justification also lies well beyond this study. Dorothea, the heroine of Eliot's *Middlemarch*, thinks dismissively about her sister Cecelia as being "hardly more in need of salvation than a squirrel" (I.4, 58). The person of faith holds himself accountable for his thoughts, his actions, his very being. Kant's notion of worthiness to be happy applies to the person of faith. Kant's worthy person is one who is consistent, free from contradiction. The person of faith may not always discern his worthiness according to merit or grace, and

Augustine in his anti-Pelagian writings would counsel against any attempt to ascertain worthiness according to merit.

Holding oneself accountable may be linked to desiring a reward, but if so, the reward is of the most sublime sort, a desire to be right, to be justified. Calvin's notion of justification expresses this worthiness negatively: "To justify ... is nothing else than to acquit from the charge of guilt, as if innocence were proved" (*Institutes* III.11, S.3, 476). The person of faith, along with Don Quixote's knight, desires that his service be accepted by the object of faith, that his faithfulness be acknowledged. This is justification.

The individual does not have a personal relation with the non-person gods: no *I-Thou* there. With the person gods, however, the individual attempts to maintain a relationship with a being with whom he shares characteristics or at least fancies so. Buber argues that the pre-Hellenic Jew saw things differently, having a relationship with "One who cannot be represented" (*Two Types of Faith* 131). Hence the Second Commandment forbidding graven images. He attributes to Paul a radical refashioning of the notion of "made in the image and likeness." Buber asserts that the Christian God is both represented and not represented in image. The new image is Jesus Christ. Paul writes: "He is the image of the invisible God, the first-born of all creation" (Col. 1:15). Jesus the man is both imagined and known, as Augustine argues in *De trinitate*. Jesus the Christ is another matter.

Regardless of who made whom, one, man or God, is made in the image of the other. The person of faith then thinks, perhaps tacitly, that he is worthy of the faith relationship, at least to the extent that he and God possess common characteristics. In Isaiah we read: "But now thus says the LORD, he who created you, O Jacob, he who formed you, O Israel: 'Fear not, for I have redeemed you; I have called you by name, you are mine'" (43:1). Not only has the LORD made Jacob, he has renamed him "Israel" (Gen. 35:10) and continues to claim possession of him. The concern of those who decry the tyranny of the Judeo-Christian God seems minor in comparison with Isaiah where we find a stronger relationship, ownership. The person of faith seeks to be claimed by the god. He desires to be desired, to be owned, to be worthy of being held accountable. (Melville's Ahab, despite his rage, desires to be worthy of the whale, to be accorded a second meeting, which ultimately is granted to him, albeit in an extraordinary way.)

We see a clear contrast in the mode of inquiry between someone who assumes a personal relationship and one who does not. For example, consider the treatments of time by Aristotle in *Physics* (IV.10–14) and Augustine in *Confessions* (X–XIII). The former is addressed to no one; the latter begins "May I know you, who know me."

With impersonal gods such as beauty, nation, or reason, the individual stands on one side. The personal relationship is one-sided. But self-respect and accountability play a role. The desire to be right stands paramount, to know the truth, to be justified. The individual is in a way reflected into the other side of the relationship, holding one place in person and the other in likeness (Aphrodite, Uncle Sam, Apollo).

The second respect with which I consider the individual may not be especially remarkable if we have an ordinary, flesh and blood individual in mind. Let us say a lover. If we conceive of the beloved in exalted, perhaps even deified terms, our relationship becomes more complex. Now we are comparing our own characteristics with similar ones in the other person, but also contrasting our own finitude and limitations with perfections and the infinite in the beloved. We are at the brink of analogical speech about the beloved.

In a reversal of the process of deifying the beloved, there are numerous examples of gods and men conjoining to produce demi-gods such as Dionysus. The most remarkable union of this sort is the birth of Jesus Christ, the most demanding and complex of such unions of God and man. Let us assume the story of Christ.

Think of the Son of God, the son of the father. Immediately our thoughts are in the realm of persons and familial relations. More particularly we think of one son, an individual, possessing dual natures, that of God and that of man, even if when pressed on the matter we can say little about the nature of God and ultimately may be forced to repudiate entirely the notion of nature. And to be absolutely specific, we think of the Son of God as Jesus of Nazareth.

The creator became not just creation but in fact a creature, one. God, the Word, the Son of God did not enter the world as humanity or mankind, not as Spirit coursing over the land in a sloppy kenosis. The Son of God did not become man, he became a man, an individual with a time and a place, an address. It does not matter that the Word became flesh as a man or a woman, that the birth took place about 2,100 years ago or at some other time, that it occurred in Bethlehem rather than Tokyo or a village in Patagonia. Regardless of time or location, the creator truly humbled himself. He could have abdicated, i.e., quit being God. The creator could have transformed his individuality into totality. God could have become mankind, the ultimate emptying out. But rather than this face-saving move, the Son of God became an individual human being, and in so doing he ruptured time. "Just as he accepted slavery, so he accepted time" (Augustine, *Enarrationes* 74.5).

With the particularity of becoming Jesus Christ, the Son of God thoroughly confused time with the eternal. The fusing of the eternal with time is for the temporal, a fusion that is ours no matter how much it perplexes us. We have seen this particularity of Jesus Christ represented by Barth as "the point where the unknown world cuts the known world," and as "the plane which lies beyond our comprehension" and intersects our plane vertically from above (*Epistle* 29–30). A plane or surface—Jesus Christ—cuts our plane of human experience, thereby producing a line. Our understanding is confined to the line in our plane. About the plane or surface itself, we remain ignorant except that its being be revealed to us. All of Kierkegaard's *Philosophical Fragments* is devoted to this problem, summarized in the epigrammatic questions in that work. "Can a historical point of departure be given for an eternal consciousness; how can such a point of departure be of more than historical interest; can an eternal happiness be built on historical knowledge?" The point stands at the nexus of time and eternity, and because of its location we confound the two. This is Barth's ungodliness in our relationship to God (*Epistle* 44).

As confusing as the Christ proposition seems, it is not entirely foreign. Individual and temporal beings know something about the eternal. We touch it. We have access to the eternal. We know some truths, perhaps very few and largely of a logical or mathematical sort, but, nonetheless, we are acquainted with the eternal. This is not to claim that the Incarnation makes sense. It certainly does not.

According to some Christian theology (Barth), the person is further individuated in Christ. This comes about in particular through Christ's union with each one of us. Paul writes: "For as many of you as were baptized into Christ have put on Christ. There is neither Jew nor Greek, there is neither slave nor free, there is neither male nor female; for you are all one in Christ Jesus" (Gal. 3:27-8). A common interpretation of this passage is that the followers of Jesus Christ are unified in purpose. They are one as members of a team, Team Christian. The suggestion here, however, is not a unity in which one loses individuality but rather a union by which the individual is made completely one, integral, one in Christ.

To escape momentarily the nonsense of the Incarnation, let us return to the image and likeness, gods and men. We become students of mankind, of the species *Homo sapiens*. We think about the gods in Homer's works. How human they seem. Gods made in the image and likeness of men. We students of the history of man, of beauty, of the unfolding of ideas in the world find our creative ability concentrated in Homer. But not only in Homer, for there is the Bible. The petty gods of Homer have been amalgamated, unified, and enhanced. Beginning with the God who created Adam and Eve, who was the LORD to Abraham and his descendants, who later became the Father of the Son of God, we have created the omni-God in our image and likeness. This is interesting. But is it not much more interesting if we turn this anthropological story on its head? Now one might say that we are in the realm of the incredible, by which we mean the opposite of what we say. For now we are in the realm of foolishness, a realm in which belief is an alternative to either puzzlement or rejection. Reason must be grabbed and strangled (Barth). As incredible as the story may be, let me emphasize here that it revolves around individuals, but these individuals, as far as we know, remain rational beings.

8

Heaven and Rewards

There is no such thing as perfect faith. No human being can conceivably remain perfectly faithful and true. Aquinas claims that we need a life-long, continuous infusion of grace to remain perfectly faithful (*Summa theologica* II.1, Q.109, A.8–10). The appeal to grace is explicit recognition of my conclusion regarding perfect faith. We have since considered great moments in faith, in particular those involving Abraham, but they were moments. In the discussion of idolatry, we saw along with Augustine and Luther that no one can keep God's First Commandment. These authors, following Paul, expand the notion of idolatry to include the substitution of any object of faith other than the true object. Thus a consideration here of heaven and what might be called the rewards promised to the faithful seems like a concession to our finitude and imperfection, incentive to reduce our hypocrisy and idolatry.

I use the word "reward" loosely in an appeal to the notion of something received for something, quid pro quo. But I hasten to add two caveats. First, I do not claim that what is received has been earned by the recipient. Such an assertion would resolve or decide the matter of faith and works. Several of our authors argue vehemently against the notion of meritorious faith, or more precisely faith as an achievement accomplished by means of performing deeds (Paul, Augustine, Luther, Calvin, Barth). About this matter I remain puzzled, and this very puzzlement is the impetus for my entire inquiry. But salvation is promised to the faithful, and accordingly the truly faithful person receives something for something, a condition for a condition.

Second, by reward I do not mean to imply that what is received comes later in time. Here I break with the authors just cited who have much to say about perseverance. Along with Jesus, I propose that the reward is eternal, eternal life. The reward is a-temporal. In strict terms of time, it does not come before or after anything. The person of faith seeks to live a devoted and trustworthy life, and the promise of Jesus may be, in a way, in exchange for that faithfulness. But the reward is not rendered upon completion of the work.

As an addendum to these caveats I note that the eternal reward is not, strictly speaking, a motivating factor to believe, the numerous biblical claims to the contrary notwithstanding. Although "eternal life" seems to be desirous (the phrase has a nice ring to it), this ultimate satisfaction cannot motivate us to believe. Satisfaction can and necessarily does quell desire. By means of reason and experience we can fashion various ways of achieving satisfaction, of fulfilling our desires. We refer to the thoughtful and experienced person as prudent regarding his actions. But these actions are not sure evidence of belief, or of a faithful life.

Although one might describe a beautiful object as heavenly or a loving relationship as paradise, in these descriptions "heaven" and "paradise" are used metaphorically, as if a conversation were being held between two people, both of whom knew what they were talking about, heaven and paradise. Let us here consider the reward for faith in Jesus Christ, Kierkegaard's "eternal happiness" (*Postscript* 16–17). But about the achievement of a faithful life, Kierkegaard adds that "the task is ideal and maybe no one ever fulfills it" (*Postscript* 362). Furthermore, Kierkegaard has little to say about "eternal happiness." I have considered eternity in Chapter 2. As for happiness, it was seen in the previous chapter that the person of faith seeks to be worthy of it.

I have also suggested along with Don Quixote that mere acceptance or acknowledgment of faithful service may be the reward for faith. Such acknowledgment amounts to justification. The person of faith has had his faithfulness confirmed. He is right, justified, and he knows it. This is not worldly knowledge, nor is it knowledge beheld by persons of this world.

Jesus has promised eternal life to his faithful (Jn 17:1-3), knowledge of God the father and of Jesus Christ. Thus the reward is knowledge or Augustine's wisdom, which according to Aquinas is man's highest happiness (*Summa theologica* I, Q.12, A.1). But Aquinas goes on to acknowledge that fallen man, with his corrupt and disordered nature, is incapable of meriting eternal life without grace. Eternal life is out of reach for fallen, temporal man who cannot merit such a reward regardless of his faithfulness and works. He is in need of grace to accomplish the infinite (*Summa theologica* II.i, Q.109, A.5). Similarly, knowledge is the reward for other kinds of faith, although one probably would not describe this knowledge as man's "ultimate beatitude."

Thus the specific goal of the act of faith is knowledge. Aquinas and Calvin counsel here that the certainty of the knowledge depends upon the object. Thus the knowledge sought by the investor in gold or the patriot depends upon the value of gold and of the country. Knowledge may vary not only according to certainty but also according to kind, and there even may be goals or rewards for the faithful other than knowledge.

Kierkegaard disagrees with this assessment, at least with respect to "eternal happiness [which] *can be defined solely by the mode of acquisition*, whereas other goods, precisely because the mode of acquisition is accidental, or at any rate relatively dialectical, must be defined by the good itself" (*Postscript* 358). Kierkegaard goes on to cite money and knowledge as examples of goods indifferent to acquisition. One can work and save to acquire money or be born wealthy. In either case, the goodness of the money resides in the thing itself, not in the effort to acquire it. He makes the same claims regarding knowledge, which is "obtainable according to talent and external circumstances, and therefore cannot be defined solely by the mode of acquisition" (*Postscript* 358). We should distinguish here between information and the kind of knowledge or wisdom that we are considering. Some people are born with a greater capacity to learn and acquire knowledge than others, but is this the kind of knowledge promised by Jesus? Presumably people are not born with this knowledge. Is one person born with a greater capacity to acquire eternal life than another person?

If, by greater capacity, we mean possessing a greater albeit finite ability to accumulate in time an infinite and eternal knowledge, then we can confidently answer "no." This doubtless is Kierkegaard's intent when he defines the good "solely by the mode of acquisition." There is, however, wide variety among people as to their ability to accumulate what we assert to be non-temporal truths such as those of mathematics. Does one who is good at math behold in this life more of the beatific vision than one who is poor at math? Is he relieved from some of the hellish waiting that others must endure?

Although mathematics provides us with numerous examples of non-temporal truths or facts, one must wonder if this constitutes knowledge of "thee the only true God." If so, then we may have reduced God ultimately to logic. Such a reduction may seem to be ridiculous, but there is a similarity in the role or position of the unconditioned in both traditional Judeo-Christian theology and in Kant's systematic morality. In one case the unconditioned is called *God* and in the other case *reason*. But even if math proves to be a poor example, the question stands regarding greater and lesser capacity. Another version of this question is to ask if faith is a gift given to some and not to others, or perhaps more abundantly to some than to others. (Augustine goes on at length about the variety of perseverance among individuals, and Aquinas maintains that some intellects can see the essence of God more perfectly than others [*Summa theologica* I, Q.12, A.6].)

Some people seem to have great confidence that their lover is faithful, regardless of empirical evidence to the contrary (lipstick on the collar). The gift of faith, if it is a gift, can no more be ascertained and verified accurately than can the object of faith be obtained in this life. Not at all. I have acknowledged the necessity of accumulating evidence of the trustworthiness of the object of faith, and I have wondered about the tipping point, perhaps occurring at a moment (Augustine) at which evidence seems to be transformed into faith. Ultimately, however, we are in no position to explain why one person believes and another does not. Let us now consider rewards other than knowledge.

Upon being notified by the angel Gabriel that he and his wife Elizabeth were to have a son, Zechariah responded: "How shall I know this? For I am an old man, and my wife is advanced in years" (Lk. 1:18). For his doubt, the angel struck him dumb, but when his son John the Baptist was born, Zechariah regained his speech and foretold regarding his son, "you will go before the Lord to prepare his ways, to give knowledge (γνῶσιν) of salvation to his people in the forgiveness of their sins" (Lk. 1:76-7). Salvation then consists in the forgiveness of sins, the reward of faith consisting in absolution, although even in this case John the Baptist is to give knowledge of salvation. Calvin denotes this condition of forgiveness as justification (*Institutes* III.11). "To justify ... is nothing else than to acquit from the charge of guilt, as if innocence were proved" (*Institutes* S.3, 476). But for those "born OK the first time," justification will be of no significance. There is no guilt of sin to be absolved from because we are no longer in the realm of religion, i.e., sin.

Although we have observed symptoms of mankind's condition, in particular ignorance and anxiety, we have yet to address the condition from a theological point of view, at least when considered apart from faith. In other words, why is there a need for justification? I postpone these comments on original sin until the next chapter. Note, however, that justification (δικαιοσύνη) can mean simply being right, being in accord with the way things are, the truth. Is not this the highest form of knowledge?

In addition to knowledge and reconciliation or absolution, rest is offered as a reward for faithfulness. Psalm 95 speaks of those people who have hardened their hearts against the LORD: "'They are a people who err in heart, and they do not regard my ways.' Therefore I swore in my anger that they should not enter my rest" (10–11). At the beginning of *Confessions*, Augustine writes "our heart is restless until it rests in you" (I.i.1). At the end we read that Scripture:

> foretells for us that after our works which, because they are your gift to us, are very good, we also may rest in you for the Sabbath of eternal life. There also you will rest in us, just as now you work in us ... But you, Lord are always working and always at rest. Your seeing is not in time, your movement is not in time, and your rest is not in time. Yet your acting causes us to see things in time, time itself, and the repose which is outside time. (Augustine, *Confessions* XIII.xxxvi–xxxvii.51–2)

The Sabbath rest is similar to that which, according to Kant, reason seeks. "Reason, therefore, restlessly seeks the unconditionally necessary" (*Grounding* 62). The Sabbath rest is decidedly not inactive; it is contemplative for those whose hearts are not hardened.

The rest described by Augustine initially does not seem to be like the knowledge described by Aquinas. It is a relief from restlessness, an end to the perpetual struggle, to the choking of faith. It is a resolution to the inherently contradictory life of the faithful. Augustine specifies that this rest is not in time. He claims that the Lord's acting causes us to see the repose that is outside of time, by which he means that which is revealed to us in Scripture. The rest consists of resolution, which can come about only with the acquisition of knowledge.

In an attempt to understand the Sabbath rest, I refer to what appears to be its opposite, at least by worldly standards: work. I refashion a distinction drawn by Frederick Engels in Karl Marx's *Capital* between the words "labor" and "work" (I.I.2, 53, n. 1). Labor refers to the tedious, enervating effort that is required of us simply to do a job, to survive. Labor has no edifying or ennobling aspects, and although it is necessary for life, it merely drains life out of us. It is almost entirely unproductive. (Excluded here is one remarkable exception: the use of the term "labor" to refer to the action of childbirth.) Having labored, one needs to recoup, to restore one's energy and life. This recovery consists of nourishment, rest, and entertainment. If the recovery is successful, the laborer is almost in the same position as he was before he began laboring, but certainly he is no better off. And the clock is running. His recoveries will not improve with age. The labor of his life will grind him down inexorably.

As distinct from labor, consider work. Work makes the same physical demands upon the worker, drains energy as does labor, and leaves the worker in a physical state no better than the exhausted laborer. The worker is in need of physical recovery. But he differs from the laborer in this significant way. His work is personally constructive. By it he becomes ennobled and rejuvenated. The worker is made better by the work, because his activity as a worker pertains to his soul. I do not go so far as to claim that the worker makes himself into who he is, but he does work on what he has been given.

With this distinction in mind, I claim that when someone enters into the Sabbath rest he "ceases from his labors." His real work, however, is just beginning, work consisting of the beatific vision. In such a state, our seeing will not be in time, our movement will not be in time, and our rest will not be in time.

Seeing, moving, and even resting, as commonly understood, are all temporal activities. Thus, from this consideration of the Sabbath rest, from this perspective, yet again we are attempting to simulate the Incarnation in reverse. According to the language of rest, rather than rupturing time by introducing the eternal into it, we endeavor to insert time into the eternal.

Heidegger's reifying (*Being and Time* H487) is Augustine's rest. But for Heidegger it is temptation, whereas for Augustine it is the reward or completion of faith, knowledge. Eternal rest grant unto them, O Lord. Eternal happiness, eternal life, total absolution, rest outside of time: these rewards appeal to us in a way, but in another way they are entirely foreign to our being. As temporal, desirous creatures with memory, can we possibly conceive of a reward devoid of these characteristics? In Marilynne Robinson's *Gilead*, the narrator, an aging minister, speaks about his friend, again another minister: "Boughton says he has more ideas about heaven every day. He said, 'Mainly I just think about the splendors of the world and multiply by two. I'd multiply by ten or twelve if I had the energy. But two is much more than sufficient for my purposes'" (147).

Augustine claims: "It is clear, then, that felicity consists in the full attainment of all desirable things" (*City of God* V, Preface). Anselm asserts as much in the *Proslogium* (XXV), where he claims that in the heavenly state we shall have what we desire. He continues with examples: beauty, wisdom, power, true security. This is not the heaven of the syllogism, but one of plenitude.

A world of desire necessarily banishes eternity and reintroduces time. What if the reward for faith were to be the New Jerusalem of Hobbes? Desire, then satisfaction, then more desire, then more satisfaction. It would be perhaps like the garden in *Paradise Lost*, paradise with tension. Carried to an extreme, to the Hobbesian limit, each desire would be satisfied instantly and completely in such a way that the desire would not really exist. No desire, no time, eternity.

Perhaps another way to characterize heaven is satisfaction without desire. Such a notion seems to be inherently contradictory, but that may be so in part because one thinks of heaven as a place or a state with properties. The contradiction obtains when we think of someone as being in a state of satisfaction or joy such that there is no desire or sorrow. I seek to describe, or more realistically merely to point to, an eternal condition, one for which time is not. Thus I propose the condition of satisfaction or the condition of joy, which is Augustine's rest.

Before concluding this section, let us return to knowledge and wisdom. If these terms seem too static for heavenly rewards, we have Augustine's other formulation, contemplation (*De trinitate* I.8.17, 81). Might not mathematical knowing be akin to the beatific vision? Think of the number *e*. Think of the proposition: there are infinitely many prime numbers.

9

Religion and Fellowship

According to the Acts of the Apostles, early Christians formed a close community, seeking fellowship (2:44). "Now the company of those who believed were of one heart and soul, and no one said that any of the things which he possessed was his own, but they had everything in common" (Acts 4:32). The early Christians organized themselves according to a common purpose and belief. The organization therefore was religious in that its members identified themselves as such according to their relationship to God and to Jesus Christ.

The early Christians also established rites. Paul writes to the Corinthians about participation (κοινωνία) in the body and blood of Christ (1 Cor. 10:16). These rites are works, acts to be repeated by the faithful. Early Christian religion included ritual. Thus the very establishment of Christianity extended beyond the narrow confines of the relationship of creator to creature. The early Christians performed acts that signified the relationship without necessarily being the relationship itself.

Paul also envisioned the disciples of Christ as a church. He advises the leaders of the group at Ephesus "to care for the church of God which he obtained with the blood of his own" (Acts 20:28; Eph. 1:22-3). In several places, Paul develops what appears to be a metaphor, i.e., the church is the body of Christ (1 Cor. 12:12-26; Col. 1:18, 3:14-15). The members of this church are one in Jesus Christ just as the Son of God as human being is one with each member. The unity of membership indicates a human solidarity, a relationship of individual human beings to one another: fellow Christians.

Earlier I asked if religion could help to relieve the anxiety that produces works. The tentative assessment there was bleak. I inquired further if one could give oneself a sign, perhaps by participating in religious fellowship. The assessment then, albeit tentative, was equally bleak, and our faith was reduced to merely believing that one believed. Having developed the notion of faith as inherently contradictory in its mode and objective, it is difficult not to be pessimistic about the roles played by religion and fellowship in the life of a person of faith. Such a disposition runs counter to widely held opinions about religion, at least among the practitioners, and so it behooves me to consider claims for the efficacy of religion. Does the intent of the participants, not merely to band together with like-minded people but rather to express their faith in God, primarily by means of praise, supersede the more obvious benefits of socializing with others?

That individuals, acting under religious mandates, will perform actions contrary to prevailing or current ethical norms seems to be hardly worth mentioning. Abraham was willing to sacrifice Isaac, whom he loved, because the LORD commanded it. The perpetrators of the terrorist attack against the United States on September 11, 2001 were motivated by religious zeal. Religious fanatics invariably will be condemned by the people, by us, especially when their behavior is unethical, but also when they act contrary to custom.

We are looking at religion, however, not to find worldly or even ethical justification for action but rather to seek comfort for the person of faith, to help him cope with the anxiety that must accompany his pursuit. Pope Francis argues on behalf of the efficacy of Christian religion. The Christian allows Christ to dwell in his heart (Eph. 3:17), and in so doing takes on the loving perspective of Jesus (Francis, *Lumen fidei* I.21). This perspective is both relational and broadening, and it necessarily includes others. "In this way, the life of the believer becomes an ecclesial existence, a life lived in the Church" (*Lumen fidei* I.22). "Faith is not a private matter," but rather one that includes verbal expression and proclamation (*Lumen fidei* I.22; cf. Rom. 10:10).

For Francis, faith is not only communal and relational in the present but also historically: faith is passed on, in a way, from person to person (*Lumen fidei* III.37–8). I presume that Francis is not arguing that contact is a sufficient condition for the transmission of faith but merely a necessary one, one that is necessary for the fulfillment of the individual. "Self-knowledge is only possible when we share in a greater memory. The same thing holds true for faith, which brings human understanding to its fullness" (*Lumen fidei* III.38). He concludes: "It is impossible to believe on our own" (*Lumen fidei* III.39).

Faith or trust does not occur without foundation, not without some evidence of trustworthiness. One does not learn about the object of faith without a sign, without some sort of revelation. When individuals who profess to be believers are asked from whom or where they obtained their faith, they often cite other individuals, usually parents, other family members, or friends. Augustine had Monica. Parents may not be the ultimate or genuine source of faith— if they are, they are highly inconsistent in this regard, imparting faith to one child and not to another—but they are necessary, they or some other means of revelation.

Is this of any help? The believer's anxiety, we saw, is rooted in time. The objective of faith is knowledge, or perhaps one should say truth, eternal. The mode of believing consists of pursuing and waiting, constantly in a state of ignorance, in a state of untruth, choking yet persevering. Although contact may have been necessary for the condition of faith to arise in the first place, I ask what good can it do henceforth.

We have countless testimonials to the efficacy of faith. These testimonials occur in fine literature, on television, and among friends, acquaintances, and strangers. They speak on behalf of the community of the faithful, that it assists in our daily life. Fellowship lightens the burden of living. This may seem to claim no more than that we are social beings. Most of us, most of the time, thrive when we have some human contact.

Of course, for the non-believer, religion might make life much more difficult. Consider the terrorist attack of September 11, 2001. And even for the believer religion may be an obstacle. But we seek here religion's beneficial properties. Are there special characteristics of a faith community that are enhanced by fellowship and that are not found in social groups organized around some principle other than faith?

Paul Tillich and others have framed this question historically. Tillich sees a transformation from medieval to modern times, from guilt and grace felt communally to a state of personal responsibility (*Courage* 87–8, 144–5). Without denying the role that the environment plays on the person, the significance of historical context, I have characterized the problem of faith (responsibility) as ahistorical, or all historical. The contradiction of faith occurs in life, in time, in the demand for perseverance. The need for the hypocrite and idolater to recommit is ever present. This recommitment is supposedly made possible by grace. Faith occurs in this world. It is relational. We might say that the person of faith has a human problem, one for which one might seek a human remedy. Such a remedy may be religious fellowship. It lightens the burden for some. If so, it operates on a human scale, temporally, ever fading and ever in need of renewal. No one can get enough of it. But in the realm of existence, existing is of great significance. Temporal balm for a temporal wound. This much and a continuous infusion of grace should suffice.

I am inclined to agree with Karl Barth, who severely limits the effectiveness of religious fellowship. "Genuine fellowship is grounded upon a negative: it is grounded upon what men lack." As sinners, we are brothers (*Epistle* 101). When men boast of faith as "some achievement of men, the divine operation in faith is ended, and is degraded to a worthless and transitory thing of this world" (*Epistle* 59).

Religion and its fellowship will not provide the knowledge sought by the person of faith, nor the justification sought by Calvin, nor the rest sought by Augustine. At best, religion is a sign pointing to the object of faith. It is revelatory. At best, the fellowship that attends religion supports the person of faith to persevere in the face of his hypocrisy and idolatry.

I seek here to show only the limits of religious fellowship in addressing the anxiety of faith. It is conceivable, however, that a religion would claim to possess a divine balm or lubricant, a charism that transcends the divide between the temporal world and the eternal, and further to claim to be able to impart this transcendence: a sacrament. In short, a religion or church may claim to possess grace and to be able to dispense or withhold it. Were the person of faith able to know of such possession and dispensing, without recourse to yet an additional layer of belief, then his anxious condition may be truly ameliorated. But the possession by human beings of grace or grace dispensaries which they in turn impart to others surely is a matter of faith. Thus the claim to sacrament alters in no way the condition of the person of faith. He still must believe in order to see: "faith seeking understanding."

It may seem blasphemous and trivial to recommend religion for its social benefits. The blasphemy arises by reducing to an emotional crutch that which religion might consider as its only connection to the truth: that it points to it. And it is commonplace to observe that people join organizations in order to meet other people, to combat loneliness. What kind of disease is loneliness?

ORIGINAL SIN AND LONELINESS

In his treatment of original sin, Calvin begins by noting indirectly the famous inscription at the temple of Apollo at Delphi: "Know thyself!" (*Institutes* II.1, S.1, 147). Calvin refers to Augustine's claim that pride stands at the beginning of all evil and Calvin extends this notion to include infidelity. In his discussion of Adam and Eve in the garden, he asserts that infidelity stands "at the root of the revolt" from which pride, ingratitude, and other sins come (*Institutes* 4, 149). Estrangement of Adam from his maker led to the death of his soul (*Institutes* 5, 150). Because of their betrayal, Adam and Eve lost their "heavenly ornaments" of wisdom, virtue, justice, truth, and holiness, and this corruption proved to be hereditary. This inheritance is universal, so much so as to become original. And although the sin referred to here is inextricably connected to time, it is not a temporal inheritance, a curse that is passed down from parents to their children.

Calvin again quotes Augustine (*De gratia Christi*): "Both the condemned unbeliever and the acquitted believer beget offspring not acquitted but condemned, because the nature which begets is corrupt" (*Institutes* II.1, S.7, 152). Calvin warns that we, the children, are not innocent and blameless inheritors of our iniquitous parents. Augustine calls the fall a double death. "We ... were dead in both body and soul—in soul because of sin, in body because of sin's punishment; and thus in *body* too *because of sin*" (*De trinitate* IV.3.5, 156). The defilement of our nature is complete. Augustine also connects the fall with the Delphic mandate. He claims that fallen man is incapable of maintaining attention upon his inner self which contains beauties. Rather than this, the mind "slithers and slides down into less and less which is imagined to be more and more." It falls in love with things that are bodies and that are outside itself. In short, it is distracted (*De trinitate* X.5.7, 293).

We are fallen; we find ourselves to be as we are in this world. It is a state of inauthenticity. Heidegger also describes the condition as fallenness (Verfallenheit) (*Being and Time* H175). He goes to some length, however, to attempt to distinguish his fallenness from that of Augustine and Calvin. The condition for Heidegger is strictly a condition of *Dasein*, a condition of existence (*Being and Time* H179–80, 234). My concern here is simply to point to a characteristic of original sin—loneliness—and a fuller treatment of the matter must await another time and place. I note, however, that the distinction that Heidegger is eager to maintain may not be at all. Existence may well be the qualification of sin that makes it original.

Paul has a broad notion of what constitutes the flesh (σάρξ). He writes: "For I know that nothing good dwells within me, that is, in my flesh" (Rom. 7:18). Paul argues that the Spirit and the flesh "are opposed to one another" (Gal. 5:17), and in giving examples of works of the flesh, Paul cites not only fornication and impurity, but also idolatry, sorcery, enmity, strife, jealousy, anger, selfishness, dissension, party spirit, and envy (Gal. 5:19-20).

In recalling a daughter who died in infancy many decades ago, the aging Reverend Ames of Robinson's *Gilead* observes: "Any human face is a claim on you, because you can't help but understand the singularity of it, the courage and loneliness of it" (66). The eyes of the face speak both of uniqueness and of isolation, of separation, of an abyss yearning to be filled. Is this any different from the guilt of the sinner who according to Calvin is in need of justification?

Loneliness may seem to be too weak a notion to describe the fallen condition, the condition of original sin. But Calvin, relying on Augustine, calls the condition an estrangement. We see the loneliness referred to by Reverend Ames not only in the eyes of strangers but also in the eyes of our dearest friends. Surely there are those among us who acknowledge, or deny, to greater or lesser degree, the estrangement of their condition. It seems that circumstance and surroundings can aggravate or ameliorate the condition. But nothing eradicates it. Paul writes: "We know that the whole creation has been groaning in travail together until now; and not only the creation, but we ourselves ... groan inwardly as we await for adoption as sons" (Rom. 8:22-3). The loneliness of the orphan is original, and its degradation is sinful. Loneliness is not the sole manifestation of original sin, but it is good evidence. There is additional evidence of fallenness, in particular: time as both an inner condition for experience and an outer phenomenon, an alien, a suffering.

Regarding loneliness, Milton apparently concurs. In his telling of the story of Adam and Eve and of the Fall, he depicts Eve's deliberations after she has eaten the fruit but before she has spoken to Adam. One of her fears is that she will be punished by God for her transgression with death, whereas the unfallen Adam might receive a new Eve in her place. Her fear, however, is more complex than mere jealousy. She concludes: "So dear I love him, that with him all deaths/I could endure, without him live no life" (Milton, *Paradise Lost* IX.832–3). Abandonment, not death, is Eve's real fear.

Eve informs Adam of her sin, and although he is greatly dismayed, he joins her. "How can I live without thee, how forgo/Thy sweet converse and love so dearly joined … ?" (*Paradise Lost* IX.906–10). Taking the fruit and God's prohibition literally, to eat of it is to sin. Under my interpretation, Adam suffers the consequence of sin in anticipation of its commission. Adam fears, as does Eve, being forsaken, even in righteousness. Adam chooses sin and death in preference to what he deems to be abandonment, estrangement, loneliness. In *Paradise Lost* Adam and Eve suffer the consequence of their sin before they commit it. One might say they were fallen from the beginning.

According to Paul, "the wages of sin is death" (Rom. 6:23). When I look at the death of Jesus Christ, whom God made "to be sin who knew no sin" (2 Cor. 5:21), I find additional support for this interpretation of original sin. Jesus, at least according to Matthew (27:46) and Mark (15:34), quotes the beginning of Psalm 22 in his final, dying exclamation: "My God, my God, why hast thou forsaken me?" Perhaps fear of death, the wage of sin, is implied in this cry, but explicitly Jesus expresses fear of abandonment, of being forsaken, of loneliness.

In looking into the eyes of his infant daughter, Reverend Ames saw a claim on himself, what I call an abyss. Religion cannot fill the gap, which is infinitely wide. Religion can neither reconcile nor justify. Religion can only tempt, confusing the temporal with the eternal. Nevertheless, the faithful, by which I mean the hypocrites and idolaters, have chosen to live a life of contradiction, one in which they must continuously reaffirm their belief in the face of their own infidelity. One might even describe this continuous reaffirmation as courageous (Tillich). The faithful anticipate an infusion of grace. Do they live a life of grace? We all fear abandonment and loneliness, but perhaps the faithful person increases his burden by professing the contradictory, the absurd. And he does so over and over again, often with like-minded people. The abandoned sinner seeks fellowship, even if it is in a community of emptiness and meaninglessness, even if one surrounds oneself with friends of utility. Perhaps religion will lighten our burdens. If so, it accomplishes its feat in mundane fashion, but among us temporal beings the temptation of religion is hard to resist. Fellowship may be the best this world has to offer to counter our fallen state, our fear of death (the wrath of God) and of loneliness, both of which are expressions of time.

10

Tests of Faith

I move now to tests of faith, beginning again with the definition from Hebrews:

> Now faith is the assurance (ὑπόστασις) of things hoped for, the conviction (ἔλεγχος) of things not seen.
> Now faith is the substance (ὑπόστασις) of things desired, the testing (ἔλεγχος) of things not known for certain. (Heb. 11:1)

There are two sides to the faith relation, and we seek signs from both sides. We want to receive a sign from the object of faith that it is worthy of our trust, that it is the truth. We want also to persuade ourselves of our faithfulness, our truth and trustworthiness. We seek "the conviction (ἔλεγχος) of things not seen." I read "testing" for ἔλεγχος. And for "things seen" I equate "to see" with "to understand." Thus we seek "to test things not known for certain."

The famous tests of faith are adventitious and present themselves as external temptations. Martyrdom is an especially clear example of testing one's faith. No test, however, can be more remarkable than the LORD's trial of Abraham, commanding him to sacrifice his son Isaac. Literature, too, is full of similar tests. All of *Don Quixote* can be read as a test of faith, the test being directed both to the object, Dulcinea, and to the person of faith, Don Quixote.

Let us consider the possibility of tests that do not come from without, but rather tests that may entail to some degree the will of the individual being tested, a test (ἔλεγχος) that may be viewed as conviction. One may have wondered, as have I, when traveling along the coast that one does not see numerous mulberry trees and mountains scattered about in the sea. This unusual sight would have come about by followers of Jesus Christ who, possessing "faith as a grain of mustard seed," had decided to exercise the power conveyed to them by their faith. Such an exercise would be mere display, but it could serve as a sign for others. The gospels provide ample evidence of Jesus' willingness to employ signs. For example, having returned sight on the Sabbath to a man who was blind, Jesus was asked: "If you are the Christ, tell us plainly." Jesus answered: "The works that I do in my Father's name, they bear witness to me; but you do not believe, because you do not belong to my sheep" (Jn 10:24–6). Members of his audience prepared to stone Jesus, accusing him of blasphemy. He responded: "If I am not doing the works of my Father, then do not believe me; but if I do them, even though you do not believe me, believe [in] the works, that you may know and understand that the Father is in me and I am in the Father" (Jn 10:37-8; see also 14:1-11).

By exhorting his audience to "believe the works," presumably Jesus is not claiming that one should believe that he has indeed enabled the blind man to see. That is obvious and would require belief from only the most resolute skeptic. Rather than this, Jesus is telling his listeners to "know and understand that the Father is in me and I am in the Father." This is the knowledge that Jesus will subsequently define as eternal life (Jn 17:3). In other words, this knowledge is the reward for or culmination of faith in him, the beatific vision. This reward, we have been told, may be achieved by means of faith. (This does not mean that, by claiming to believe Jesus is the Christ, one has exhibited faith in Jesus.) Thus the works are revelation, signs pointing to the truth.

One of the most remarkable works in the New Testament is the resurrection of Jesus from the dead. Well known is the passage about Doubting Thomas, who does not believe that the other disciples have seen the risen Lord (Jn 20:24-9). When Jesus appears to Thomas, he shames him. Thomas exclaims: "My Lord and my God!" Augustine points out that Thomas did not then believe that Jesus was a living man. This he could see; he could understand it. Thomas believed that the man standing before him was his Lord and God. As Augustine writes, "he saw one thing and believed another" (*Homilies on John* "Tractate LXXIX," XIV, 29–31). Buber claims that Thomas is the first doctrinal Christian (*Two Types of Faith* 128). But Peter also should be added to the list of Christians. Not long after the miracle of the loaves and fishes,

Jesus asked his disciples: "Who do you say that I am?" Simon Peter replied: "You are the Christ, the Son of the living God" (Mt. 16:15-16). Jesus blesses Peter and then notes that Peter's understanding had not been revealed to him by human beings but by the father, i.e., I, Jesus of Nazareth, have not revealed this to you, nor could I (Mt. 16:17). Jesus underscores here the role and limit of signs. Feeding thousands with seven loaves of bread and a few small fish is truly miraculous, and thus Peter could attest to a power possessed by Jesus. The assertion, however, that Jesus is the Christ is a matter of faith and blessedness. Flesh and blood, specifically Jesus of Nazareth, could not impart this faith to Peter any more than could the multiplication of loaves and fishes. The signs point.

Thus the case for signs is made, but we are considering the possibility of giving a sign to others as well as to oneself by testing one's own faith. The biblical passages that set the scene regarding the power of faith are numerous and well known. "The apostles said to the Lord, 'Increase our Faith!' And the Lord said, 'If you had faith as a grain of mustard seed, you could say to this sycamine [mulberry] tree, 'Be rooted up, and be planted in the sea,' and it would obey you'" (Lk. 17:5-6). There is also the somewhat uncertain conclusion to the Gospel of Mark. In this passage, Jesus reprimands some of his disciples for not believing other witnesses who had seen him after he had risen.

He who believes and is baptized will be saved; but he who does not believe will be condemned. And these signs will accompany those who believe: in my name they will cast out demons; they will speak in new tongues; they will pick up serpents, and if they drink any deadly thing, it will not hurt them; they will lay their hands on the sick, and they will recover. (Mk 16: 9-18)

What is Jesus saying? You can move mountains and trees. You can safely handle deadly serpents. But should you? Should one test one's own faith? Biblical passages indicate that God himself is being put to the test when they warn against it. Moses, addressing all of Israel, commands: "You shall not put the LORD your God to the test, as you tested him at Massah" (Deut. 6:16). Upon being tempted by the devil in the wilderness, Jesus echoes the sentiment (Mt. 4:7; Lk. 4:12).

The believer is in a constant state of contradiction, struggling to accumulate that which cannot be accumulated. And yet there *are* signs. Perhaps one could give oneself a sign, could relieve some of the anxiety and doubt that accompanies faith. Kierkegaard replies that it is a temptation "to want to quantify oneself into faith" (*Postscript* 13). Yes, but it is a temptation to or for the very thing to which faith is oriented: acknowledgment by the object of faith of one's faithfulness.

It is understandable why a believer might refuse to take the test, fearing the results. What would be gained from such a test? Perhaps a small sign, but no more. Nothing definitive, just another mulberry tree in the sea. We might even find consolation in our refusal to take the test by assuring ourselves that nothing would be gained from such a test in any event. Perhaps a mark of faith is the disdain one might show for a mere display. "You shall not put the LORD your God to the test." The person of faith has already accumulated some evidence for belief: the exemplary practice of his parents; a verse from Romans; a miraculous event. But with faith there comes doubt, a struggle. We are working largely in the dark. Hence, perhaps, the need for a test.

Can one test suffice, be it adventitious or self-inflicted? Can Abraham make one trip up Mt. Moriah and be done with it, or must he ascend the mountain again each day? Might he recur to his fidelity that one time on Mt. Moriah, rebuffing any further inquiries or tests from the LORD or from himself? Can we dispense with the anxiety of faith in one fell swoop? Is faith like charity in one narrow sense, that a single act of faith may suffice in the same way that a single act of charity might?

Here is a literary example in which a single act of faith has life-long significance. Lucas Beauchamp, the protagonist in Faulkner's "The Fire and the Hearth" (*Go Down, Moses*), is a man of faith, although he is never described as such in the story. He places his faith in his grandfather, Carothers McCaslin, in his blood. Lucas was born of former slaves, who were freed a few years before his birth, and he chooses to live his long life raising corn and cotton on the very land where his parents were enslaved. In the eyes of society, he is a Negro tenant farmer. Old Carothers, his grandfather (and great-grandfather), was the white owner of the plantation. Faithful and resolute, in many ways Lucas is stupid and obstinate.

In an attempt to implicate his son-in-law George Wilkins for moonshining, Lucas is tricked by George and his daughter. When the sheriff comes to investigate, George's still is found on Lucas's property. As for Lucas's still, one of the sheriff's deputy's reports "so we set down and thought about just where would we hide a still if we was one of Mr. Roth's niggers and we went and looked there and sho enough there it was, neat and careful as you please" (*Go Down, Moses* 63). Subsequently, Lucas and George become partners in moonshining and acquire a new still. Lucas asks George where the still is located, and George responds: "I hid hit in that gully where mine used to be. Since them shurfs never found nothing there the yuther time, they'll think hit aint no use to look there no more" (*Go Down, Moses* 74). Lucas rebukes George, calling him a fool, and insists that they hide the still in a place that *he* determines to be safe.

In the course of the story, Lucas becomes obsessed with finding buried treasure on the plantation, and accordingly he neglects some of his farming duties. This neglect is coupled with an obstinate dedication to using outdated methods of tending to his crop. Roth Edmonds, the "owner" of the land, reminisces:

> There were the years during which Lucas had continued to farm his acreage in the same clumsy old fashion which Carothers McCaslin himself had probably followed, declining advice, refusing to use improved implements, refusing to let a tractor so much as cross the land which his McCaslin forbears had given him ... refusing even to allow the pilot who dusted the rest of the cotton with weevil poison, even fly his laden aeroplane through the air above it. (*Go Down, Moses* 113)

When Edmonds criticizes Lucas for wasting time hunting for buried treasure while neglecting his crops, Lucas responds: "You aint got any complaints about the way I farm my land and make my crop, have you?" (*Go Down, Moses* 116).

My interest in Lucas Beauchamp, man of faith, centers on the efficacy of a single act. Lucas recalls such a single act of faith and great courage that he performed forty-three years earlier. As he approached the main house on the land to inform Edmonds about George's still, Lucas recalled the past event. His then new wife Molly had been nursing and caring for their first-born child while doing the same for Edmonds himself. Edmonds's mother had died in childbirth, and his father Zachary had taken in Molly to care for the newborn. After nearly half a year, Lucas demanded of Zack that Molly be returned to his house. Although Molly returned, with both babies, Lucas decided that the insult was unbearable. Lucas thought, "I got to kill him [Zachary] or I got to leave here" (*Go Down, Moses* 48). Lucas confronts Zachary in his bedroom. Lucas is holding an open razor. Zachary tells him to put it down. Lucas responds:

> You knowed I wasn't afraid, because you knowed I was a McCaslin too and a man-made one. And you never thought that, because I am a McCaslin too, I wouldn't. You never even thought that, because I am a nigger too, I wouldn't dare. No. You thought that because I am a nigger I wouldn't even mind. I never figured on the razor neither. But I gave you your chance. Maybe I didn't know what I might have done when you walked in my door, but I knowed what I wanted to do, what I believed I was going to do, what Carothers McCaslin would have wanted me to do. But you didn't come. You never even gave me the chance to do what old Carothers would have told me to do. You tried to beat me. And you wont never, not even when I am hanging dead from the limb this time tomorrow with the coal oil still burning, you wont never. (*Go Down, Moses* 52)

Lucas insists that Zachary get his pistol, and eventually the two men fight over the gun. Obtaining control, Lucas "jammed the pistol against the white man's side and pulled the trigger and flung the white man from him all in one motion, hearing as he did so the light, dry, incredibly loud click of the miss-fire" (*Go Down, Moses* 56).

Lucas acted as honor and faith demanded of him. Had he not attempted to kill Zack Edmonds, he would not have been able to live with himself. Had he killed Zack Edmonds, or even wounded him, he surely would have been lynched. Lucas had prepared a second cartridge in the gun to use to kill himself if he had in fact killed Zack. Subsequently he thought: "I wouldn't have used the second one. I would have paid. I would have waited for the rope, even the coal oil. I would have paid. So I reckon I aint got old

Carothers' blood for nothing, after all. Old Carothers, I needed him and he come and spoke for me" (*Go Down, Moses* 57).

Thus ends Lucas's recollection. Perhaps he performed faithful and courageous deeds at other times in his life, but these are not part of the story. We have a single act, albeit extraordinary, from which Lucas draws his strength and to which he could point and say: "Then! There! I gave a sign of my faithfulness to Old Carothers. I did what he would have wanted me to do. I acted according to my faith in him. *And I received a sign.* Old Carothers came and spoke for me. His blood runs deservedly in me."

Like Lucas, we may find strength and sustenance by recollecting past deeds, deeds that contribute to the formation of our very being. But is not faithfulness always in jeopardy? Does it not require perseverance, similar to chastity. What would momentary or even intermittent chastity be? Not chastity. Analogously, would not momentary faith be faithlessness, betrayal, pursuit of untruth? The person of faith must persevere continually and uninterruptedly. And yet we are defined in part by individual events.

We, the faithful (i.e., the unfaithful), know that we are hypocrites and idolaters. Can this self-knowledge be combined with the recollection of some faithful moment in our past to provide a framework for life? In principle it cannot, and in fact it does. Knowledge of our hypocrisy and idolatry is clear evidence that we understand the meaning of faithfulness. The measure of our failing is a mark of that understanding of what it means to abide. Paul, Augustine, and Luther know that no one keeps the First Commandment, no one loves "the LORD his God with all his heart, and with his soul, and with all his might." Most vividly, at the moment of full realization that one is at best intermittently faithful, Augustine puts "on the Lord Jesus Christ," he places his trust in the Lord. It is in the face of his own infidelity that Augustine performs a single, momentary act of faith. Thus, by putting "on the Lord Jesus Christ," Augustine has overcome the world. He has overcome Paul's flesh. The Letter of John claims that this clothing is achieved by keeping God's commandments, which are not burdensome (5:3-5). Not burdensome? We have seen ample testimony and argument that no one keeps God's commandments. "None is righteous, no, not one" (Rom. 3:10). "All have sinned and fall short of the glory of God" (Rom. 3:23).

We can easily imagine that, upon recognizing our infidelity, we would abandon our faith. It happens all the time. Such surrender might occur from the kind of deliberations expressed here, but it might also occur as a matter of fatigue. This is what happens to Don Quixote. Alonso Quijana was an aging man to begin with, before he adopted the persona of Don Quixote. Having done so, and after repeated failures to see evidence of the good that it would bring into the world, he questioned his faith. Faith is a struggle (Calvin), a battle, and Don Quixote lost it. Literally beaten down by the Knight of the White Moon, Don Quixote became Alonso the Good, i.e., Alonso the Apostate. He gave up.

We hear in Cervantes's *Don Quijote* that we are children of our works (I.4, 39; I.47, 386; II.32, 637). At least to some extent, we make ourselves into who we are. We produce an accumulation, albeit finite. Can we make ourselves faithful through our actions? This question is similar to the one previously considered about giving oneself a sign of faith.

Mortification of the flesh, especially fasting and abstinence, is a common form of testing one's self. Most religions codify the practice. How strictly must one observe these restrictions, to what extent must the person of faith go to persuade himself that he is indeed faithful? Exemplary in this regard is the image of the emaciated St. Catherine of Siena, wearing the foreskin of the circumcised Christ on her finger as a wedding ring while surviving on a diet consisting solely of the Eucharist and of pus from rank, cancerous sores of the sick.

Let us view the problem from a different direction. When we tell ourselves that despite our best efforts we know that we shall fail in the future, that we shall neglect, waver, betray, sin, what are we saying to ourselves? Are we planning to fail again, tomorrow at noon? More likely the remark is uttered from a position of apparent abstraction. It is uttered by a student of human behavior in general and a specialist in one's own behavior. But is it mere acknowledgment of human frailty, or is it surrender?

The optimistic interpretation, the one of good intent, favors the former. It alleges that one's intention, at this moment, is to remain faithful, to shun idolatry. This is Buber's accommodation. "God expects from thee fulfilment according to thy nature and ability ... not less, but also not more" (*Two Types of Faith* 79–80). This must be John's view, too, when he claims that the Lord's "commandments are not burdensome" (1 Jn 5:3). This is a world filled with grace. But have not we all been participants in a conversation similar to this?

> But you said that you loved me.
> I meant it when I said it.

The optimistic interpretation acknowledges a past that is both idolatrous and hypocritical, and proclaims likelihood to the point of certainty that the same behavior awaits us in the future. (I recognize that this analysis is graceless, but I persist.) Acknowledgment of human frailty gives with one hand and takes away with the other.

When Jesus saved the adulterous woman from death by stoning by shaming the scribes and Pharisees (Jn 8:1-11), he said:

> Woman, where are they? Has no one condemned you?
> She said, "No one, Lord."
> And Jesus said, "Neither do I condemn you; go, and do not sin again."

Jesus did not say, "Go, and try not to sin again." He did not say:

> Admittedly human beings are frail and inconstant. Nonetheless, as you encounter temptations henceforth, you will be free to resist them and capable of resisting them. For my yoke is easy, and my burden is light. My Father will not place on you a burden greater than you can bear. That having been said, you *will* yield again to temptation. All humans yield. It is in their fallen and corrupted nature. Try not to let it get you down.

The optimistic interpretation, as I have called it, is of two minds. One, let us assume, consists of intent that is pure: to keep the faith. But this proclamation comes from a creature of experience. Does the temptation contained here come from one side, i.e., are we being tempted by time? Perhaps we are being tempted by eternity? Our confusion here is similar to our confused prayer for Judas. We are holding two positions, resolute despite their incompatibility, as if we were about to effect the Incarnation. Are we anticipating an infusion of grace? Are we tempting the LORD, attempting to force his beneficent hand?

Or do we surrender? Does the person of faith acknowledge necessarily that he is also unfaithful, that what it means to be faithful is to be unfaithful? We shall never know in this life. One might wish that Barth's and Bonhoeffer's claims about works and obedience could be stood on their heads to our advantage by applying them to our sins and vices. We can never know for certain the degree of our culpability. Such a gambit does not work. Given that knowledge is the objective of faith, the person of faith can hardly find solace or relief in ignorance. Furthermore, just as a finite accumulation will not achieve an infinite end, any blame whatsoever convicts the individual. "Go, and do not sin again."

We are capable of aspiring to greatness, to behold the beatific vision. In this very limited sense, that aspiration is sufficient to live one's life as if one truly intended to "go and not sin again." This is where Augustine stood at the moment of conversion. Momentary "assurance of things hoped for, the conviction of things not seen" helps us to move from today to tomorrow, just as religious fellowship may help us to move to the day after tomorrow. When we reflect upon these momentous resolutions, which are actions, they fade into nothingness compared to the never-ending pursuit of knowledge. We tell ourselves that we are the children of our deeds, that we have made ourselves, but in the face of choice, of life, we choke on the uncertainty of our next act, of our next intention. The individual act of the past is temporalized. It lives in our memory, but it must be continuously interpreted as present faithfulness. The uncertainty about the future amplifies the significance of the past. We might even doubt the faithfulness, the abiding of anyone who is not aghast at his own faithlessness.

I consider briefly another moment of temptation and faithfulness from literature. That the Pequod is approaching the white whale has been doubly confirmed by meetings with two other whalers (Melville, *Moby-Dick* 397, 403). Ahab, standing on deck, leans over the side of the boat and watches his shadow sink into the water. He sheds a tear into the sea. Starbuck approaches. Ahab reminisces about forty years of whaling.

> ... the desolation of solitude it has been ... oh, weariness! ... whole oceans away, from that young girl-wife I wedded past fifty, and sailed for Cape Horn the next day ... I feel deadly faint, bower, and humped, as though I were Adam, staggering beneath

the piled centuries since Paradise …. Close! Stand close to me, Starbuck; let me look into a human eye; it is better than to gaze into sea or sky; better than to gaze upon God … I see my wife and my child in thine eye. (Melville, *Moby-Dick* 405–6)

Starbuck replies, "why should any one give chase to that hated fish! Away with me! Let us fly these deadly waters! Let us home! Wife and child, too, are Starbuck's." He then calls up visions of Nantucket, "they have some such mild blue days, even as this, in Nantucket" (*Moby-Dick* 406). Ahab responds. "They have, they have. I have seen them—some summer days in the morning. About this time—yes, it is his noon nap now—the boy vivaciously wakes; sits up in bed; and his mother tells him of me, of cannibal old me; how I am abroad upon the deep, but will yet come back to dance him again" (*Moby-Dick* 406).

Fatigued like Don Quixote, indeed fatigued like old Adam crushed by the weight of all human sin, envisioning his child in Nantucket on such a "mild blue day," tempted by the ethical like Kierkegaard's Abraham, Ahab resists. The devil (Starbuck) in the wilderness (Pacific Ocean) tempts Jesus (Ahab). Ahab is tempted to replace the divine with the human, to "look into a human eye; it is … better than to gaze upon God." But Ahab keeps the faith. He pursues the truth.

Let us go back, finally, to Abraham, when God seeks to test (tempt or prove) him. On Mt. Moriah, Abraham gives a sign and he receives a sign in the form of the ram caught in the thicket to be offered up and burnt. The sign has come from the object of faith, the LORD. It substitutes for the sign that Abraham had previously received from the LORD and that he had just bound on the altar, Isaac.

We have in this scene an exemplar, a pinnacle of the faith relation. Perhaps to the greatest extent possible for a human being, Abraham has seen evidence of the LORD's care for him and has given evidence of his trustworthiness for all, including himself, to see. This he has done, presumably, at the height of anxiety, in the crucible of faith, when he attempts to sacrifice Isaac.

Having offered up the substitute ram, Abraham named the place on Mt. Moriah. "The LORD will provide; as it is said to this day, 'On the mount of the LORD it shall be provided'" (Gen. 22:14). Other translations, however, give *see* or *seen* in lieu of *provide*. Thus, "as

it is said to this day, 'On the mount of the LORD he shall be seen.'"
This latter translation accords with my treatment of *to see* as well
as with my understanding of faith as a quest for knowledge. At that
place on Mt. Moriah, Abraham obtained knowledge of the LORD,
the object of faith, as well as knowledge of himself, the obedient
believer. Thus he named the place "he shall be seen," i.e., "he shall
be known."

11

Solace, Miracles, and the Power of Prayer

Thus far we have seen that faith is a contradictory activity, an attempt to accumulate in finite bits an infinite amount, an attempt to ascertain the truth by approximation (Kierkegaard). At the nexus of faith stands confusion between time and eternity, Barth's ungodliness. The result of this confusion is anxiety, which in turn produces works. Faith invariably entails waiting, suffering under the clock, waiting in pursuit, living as a sinner, in effect, waiting in hell. It is founded on some evidence, a sign or revelation, but it is constantly on trial, under siege both externally and internally.

Given this state of affairs, how can anyone find solace in his faith? How can faith serve as a foundation for living? It would seem that the person of faith would be anything but consoled, constantly placing in jeopardy his claim to constancy, as certain of his future shortcomings as he is of his hypocritical and idolatrous past. How can consolation be found in our attempts to find firm footing on the submerged, slimy rock of faith? The person of faith continuously focuses a magnifying glass on his imperfections and corruption. (When he neglects to do so, he lets faith slip away into complacency.) He chronicles religiously the onslaught of time against his resolve. Infidelity and hypocrisy are causes of shame, if not shame before God, before a lover, or before mankind, then shame before oneself. One recognizes his own unworthiness to be happy.

I distinguish this concern from religious fellowship which, by its very nature, provides support, consolation in times of trial. (Of course, religion also excludes, discriminates, marginalizes.) I want to think about the solace that faith per se, independent of encouragement from like-minded people, provides to one who believes. Might there be refuge or consolation merely in being aware that human beings are creatures of faith, that they inherently seek to believe, to follow, to obey: in short, to look upward in hope of receiving grace?

If we turn to the Bible we shall find there, sprinkled in among the nearly continuous accounts of trial and agony, promises of peace and tranquility. Jesus himself claims at times to offer peace (along with separation of family members and strife). In his farewell address to his disciples he promises that his father will send the Counsellor, the Holy Spirit to "teach you all things." And then: "Peace I leave with you; my peace I give to you; not as the world gives do I give to you. Let not your hearts be troubled, neither let them be afraid" (Jn 14:25-31).

The disciples no doubt were fearful of what would become of them after Jesus had left. Would they keep the faith? Jesus assures them that the Holy Spirit will support them, and that he himself can give them peace. Paul echoes this sentiment. Having called God's chosen ones to put on compassion, meekness, patience, and above all, love, he writes: "And let the peace of Christ rule in your hearts, to which indeed you were called in the one body. And be thankful" (Col. 3:12-15).

Can Jesus Christ, the object of faith to the extent that he is the truth (Jn 14:6), give peace? Can we find peace in our "assurance of things hoped for," such as a faithful lover or value-preserving gold, despite "testing things not known for certain?" Perhaps we should inquire as to the nature of this peace, given in the case of Jesus Christ "not as the world gives." Is it an ironic peace? Tranquility that manifests itself as turmoil? Inner calm that has the outer appearance of anxious works? Eternity in the midst of time? Is Augustine's Sabbath rest described in Chapter 8, which is supremely active, the culmination of thinking and knowing in the contemplation of the beatific vision?

Many people of faith claim their faith to be a source of comfort, solace, or sure footing in a turbulent world. These claims are usually made in contrast to the discomfort and unhappiness brought on by external, earthly events. There even may be an element of bravado in such claims. The braggart might exclaim: "Unlike Job, when faced with the loss of my worldly goods, I won't even ask for an

audience with God. I will trust in Him." He might say: "Unlike
Ahab, who must meet up again with the whale, I can let this go."
We hear: "In trying times, I have my faith, hope for a better day."
Rarely, if ever, does one hear claims about faith as a refuge or solace
in the face of unexpected good fortune, such as winning the lottery.
The winner may praise the Lord and express gratitude for his newly
acquired wealth, but he does not claim recourse to faith. The better
day for which he hoped has arrived.

Claims of faith as solace express optimism not only for a
justification, a righting of wrongs in the next world or next life, but
even in this life. Does the experience of the believer authenticate his
faith? A danger encountered here is to render all our theological
considerations as psychological, a rendition that I reject even in my
claim that works are the manifestation of anxiety that accompanies
faith. Can the promise of knowledge provide solace?

Protestations regarding the firmness, certainty, and security of
faith could be interpreted skeptically as evidence of the struggle, the
need to assert and reassert constantly the thing believed, the courage
to be. The claims about comfort and solace are made regarding a
world that is apparently unjust and trying. Why else would one
need support and consolation? Commercial advertisements for
services and products are constantly offering to "treat you the way
you deserve to be treated." These offers claim to rectify the wrongs
that have been perpetrated against us, the victims, to restore justice,
to make us look as young as we feel. This is at best an ambiguous
offer, and yet its appeal is apparently undeniable. Be assured that
a better existence awaits you. But according to which or to whose
standards?

Certainly, we have a deep, inner sense of justice. Everywhere we
look in this world we see what we deem to be injustice. Are these
tumultuous and distressing occurrences truly unjust? God only
knows. Does the lover who is unfaithful, who betrays the other,
perpetrate an unjust act? He does to the extent that the act is one of
betrayal. How to judge the act is the question. The person of faith
can and does believe that the end of faith is the righting of wrongs,
justification, but such belief is entirely general.

The definition of faith claims "assurance of things hoped for."
But the believer who asserts that his faith provides him comfort
and solace cannot be talking about faith per se. Faith, we know,
is a constant struggle. Life, although almost universally loved and

cherished, is uncertain and difficult. Hobbes claims that there is no such thing as tranquility because life consists of motion, desire, fear, and sensation (*Leviathan* I.7, 129-30). Thus "eternal life" in a Hobbesian sense, life everlasting, is perpetual motion, desire, and fear. Because faith is temporal, works are entailed by faith. Faith accommodates itself to restless life because faith is action.

The comfort and solace of faith must lie in the things hoped for, the object of faith: knowledge, rest, contemplation, the mere acceptance and acknowledgment of one's faithfulness, and perhaps the greatest individual desire, to be right. Faith is mischaracterized as a solution, a resolution, a state of tranquility and certitude. Rather than this, faith is vivacious. It quickens the pulse because it proclaims assurance in the face of doubt, certitude in the face of uncertainty. We all are creatures of faith, but to proclaim one's faith takes chutzpah. Thus faith looks to be courageous, and it also looks to be absurd. One thinks of Lucas Beauchamp and Ahab. It is belief in what appears to be the manifestly impossible. Faith expects grace. There is an explanation for lipstick on the collar other than infidelity on the part of the lover.

One might also find solace in the knowledge that someone cares for him, that someone has an interest and concern for his wellbeing. This is Buber's first type of faith. If loneliness truly is a manifestation of original sin, then faith or trust in someone who cares might mitigate to some degree the feeling of estrangement and abandonment. Would not there be solace to be had in the knowledge that God so loved the world that he sent his only son to save it? And if this knowledge were unattainable in life, perhaps some comfort could be extracted from belief that God cares for the world and the individual.

That the creator has an interest in his creation is not remarkable. That the eternal action would subject the Word to time, to suffering, is another matter entirely. Moloch propitiates himself once for all. This is what the Christian confesses. In so doing, he may in fact derive solace from his faith, especially provided that he does not attempt to understand how this God could care for him.

I connect my postulate to an interpretation of faith as solace or refuge. When, in the face of a calamitous event, one makes recourse to one's faith, the move may indicate assurance or conviction in a purpose or meaning for the event, a purpose that is not evident. This assurance or refuge is conceived of as providence. There is a divine rationale, unknown to us, for the occurrences of this world. God has foreseen. He has a plan which is largely, and at times of calamity or catastrophe, entirely hidden. One might exclaim that his faith is being tested. We find ourselves alongside Abraham on Mt. Moriah, after the ram has been substituted for Isaac. Abraham named the place "it shall be seen."

Belief in providence, faith as solace, entails an acceptance of my postulate. The sequence of events amounts to an unfolding of the plan, revelation in time of the eternal. God, the author of the plan, is not bound by time. But such faith, if it indeed provides solace, presumes that the unfolding is in some way to our liking. Jesus offers peace not as the world gives. Nonetheless, countless apologists attempt to extinguish the fire of Scripture only to offer us the ashes of this world.

Along with solace, the person of faith might also claim that miracles exist. A miracle is an event or action that is both highly unlikely and highly desirable. It is "hoped for," and thus it would require faith to have assurance of the thing hoped for, given its unlikeliness. This great faith is commonly expressed as belief in the power of prayer. First, let us consider the miracle itself. My definition rules out inexplicable events that are feared or hated. Let us also eliminate for now interior actions such as a change of heart, a conversion, and both the acquisition and loss of faith. For example, a charitable act is truly remarkable and perhaps miraculous.

An event that is highly unlikely is not necessarily unnatural. Some meteorological conditions, heavy snowfall in equatorial lowlands, for example, may be highly unlikely. Such events, however, are explainable by the laws of nature. A miracle, at least in the context of this study, must extend beyond these laws. It does not make sense, however, to describe a miracle as an occurrence of the impossible, a sequence of events known to be impossible. My argument rests on our ignorance of the possible, or more precisely, on the uncertainty of the meaning of possible, e.g., consider resurrection from the dead. Nonetheless, there is a connotation to the notion of impossible. I propose that salvation is impossible. Thus the faith and hope that salvation is certain comprise a clinging to and expectation of the impossible. Let us assume that salvation is not the only miracle.

In order to understand better what a miracle is, to know what is supernatural, we first would need to know what is natural. We would need to know natures, but this is a notion that I have attempted to avoid. (I have used the word "nature" in connection with Jesus Christ to refer to the transcendent Christ. I beg the indulgence of the reader in the use of nature in this regard, especially as it pertains to the divine nature of Christ. When I consider the dual nature of Christ, I mean neither to assert that Jesus Christ has a divine nature that can be comprehended, nor to claim to understand and know human nature. By the dual nature of Christ I signify solely his transcendence, specifically that which forms a bridge up and over to the other.)

In lieu of the expression "natural law," I propose *world law*, albeit stilted and artificial. By world I signify creation, or quite simply the way things are. By law I mean a decree according to which creation unfolds in time. Decree connotes that there is one who issues the decree, perhaps even that someone exists who decrees. Perhaps there is someone whose word is act. If that connotation be abhorrent, then let law signify "all that is" as it has been, is now, and will be: the being in time.

I now define a miracle as an event or action contrary to or in violation of world law. This definition may be good in general, but its significance hinges on the meaning of "world law" and, strictly speaking, it is an empty definition. It lacks content because I am unable to define it any more precisely than to say that it accounts for the temporal world. Imagine an event, a stone falling toward the center of the earth. Classical physics, quantum mechanics, and relativity may be a start to providing the desired explanation of the event. But if there is freedom, then these disciplines cannot provide a full account. The possibility of freedom also eliminates assistance from history, anthropology, sociology, and psychology.

I cannot provide the account of the falling stone. Assume it done. The account has been given. Now I say that a miracle, if such a thing exists, contravenes the world law. Jesus Christ healed the lame. A magician pulls a rabbit out of a hat. The sun stood still so that Joshua could slaughter the Amorites (Josh. 10:12-14). We are not in a position, nor shall we ever be, to verify a miraculous event. We may be in a position to believe that one has occurred.

Let us now inquire into the power and workings of prayer. There may be many reasons for prayer. One might pray because one desires to have something, or desires a particular outcome. One might pray seeking forgiveness. One might offer a prayer of thanksgiving. One might pray for theologians that their speculations not overly offend the object of their discourse. And one might pray to glorify, to praise God, the world, or beauty. I shall focus on the first kind of prayer, those offered in hopes of getting something, be it material wealth, world peace, or peace of mind.

The purpose of this kind of prayer is clear. The petitioner wants something, does not see how to get it, and therefore seeks assistance in bringing about the desired result. Let us imagine that we have a friend who has fallen ill with a life-threatening disease. Our desire is simple and clear, that our friend be restored to good health. All of medical science is called upon to assist in obtaining the desired result, but the likelihood of success is doubtful. What are we to do? I consider two cases.

First, we might say that we hope that our friend's good health be restored. Our hope or desire is perfectly clear and undiminished by the discouraging reports that we have received from the medical doctors. Our hope is unaffected by our worry and sadness. We might try to bolster our spirits by observing that living organisms are very complicated, that stranger things have happened. We hope for the outlier. But even if we lose all hope that our friend will recover, and here we use hope in a different sense than strictly desire, we still desire his recovery.

Second, we might say that we pray that our friend's good health be restored. In common parlance the first and second cases may be interchangeable, but in fact they are quite different. Now we are calling, if necessary, for the contravention of world law. We are begging that the lawful course of events be altered. We are petitioning someone with the power, with enough clout to break the law.

Thus we direct our petition to someone or something that can effect the change. At other times we might beg before our mother, our lover, or currency traders for a different kind of request. But here we direct our request to the creator, just as Joshua directed his request to the LORD. What exactly are we asking the creator to do? How can we ask God to change his mind? Precisely we ask the creator to aid in the restoration of our friend's good health. We are in the position of the humble petitioner. In a wordy version of the request, we might say: "We don't care how you do it, LORD, but we beg that you cause our friend to be healed." Our expression of disinterest in the method employed for change is both clever and evasive. We postpone our consideration of the mechanism for another time, perhaps for a time when we are no longer distraught over our friend's condition. We avoid thinking about cause and effect, about the creation. We want our friend to be restored to good health. Now, or perhaps later, in a moment of reflection, we shall inquire about the method. Are we asking for a change in creation? Are we asking the creator to change his mind, so to speak, about the way his creation unfolds in time, to interfere in his creation?

Thinking along these lines, we confuse yet again time and eternity (Barth's ungodliness), just as we did when we prayed for Judas, when we attempted to understand the Incarnation, and when we reaffirmed our faith in vowing to go and not sin again. We are begging the eternal creator to make a change in the temporal unfolding of his creation. (More bold would be to implore the creator to alter creation as it had already unfolded, to change the past.) I must be clear here that the creation and its unfolding, in the mind of the creator, does not stand before us in time, in the past. Nor is it contemporaneous, nor in the future. It is eternal.

The creation plan, so to speak, is temporal as well as spatial. It contains all space and all time. Our immediate concern, our friend's health, is largely a temporal concern. Even our discovered limitations, such as the Heisenberg principle, are temporal concerns. Although we may have access to eternal truths, we are nevertheless unable to live eternally in this life. Eternal life is the promise offered by Jesus Christ to the faithful.

Does this realization render prayer useless? If so, we are in no position to determine its inefficacy. Our prayers for Judas may be useless, just as may be our prayers to avert some calamity yet to occur, e.g., a natural disaster occurring many years from now. (My prayers to alter the past seem to have fallen on deaf ears.) Our attempts to comprehend the Incarnation may be vain, because it is ultimately nonsense. Useless, too, may be our reaffirmations of faith, our determinations to go and not sin again.

We as temporal beings are incapable of comprehending ourselves temporally, although our understanding of ourselves is largely temporal. For Hobbes, Heidegger, and many others (or for all of us most of the time), the understanding is entirely temporal. We may be able to touch the eternal, to glimpse it, but only in a manner of speaking, only while passing by it. If I speak the truth here, I do so by evasive language. What we are unable to do is to stop. Time, our existence, prevents us from doing so. The beatific vision is but a promise or hope. It is not, however, a promise or hope for the future. It is eternal.

In short, our understanding of these matters likely has no practical consequence, no moral imperative either positive or negative. We cannot conclude from these deliberations that our prayers are inefficacious. We know what a miracle is but shall never be able to identify one. We may come to know ever more deeply the significance of the Incarnation without ever understanding it. We may overcome repeatedly our doubts regarding the object of faith without ever ending the struggle.

12

Crucifixion and Resurrection

Who died on the cross? This question deserves its own, independent study. My remarks may be seen as prolegomena to such a study. This question is central to my inquiry for the following reasons. Faith in the Christian God necessarily entails belief that Jesus of Nazareth, a man, is also God. But, given Augustine's notion of time as God's creation *ex nihilo* and my ensuing postulate in Chapter 1, it becomes incumbent on me to address the status of this man-God. In fairness to the question, it might seem more proper to ask: what died on the cross? I propose a taxonomy of sacrifice and martyrdom. Our two fundamental categories are human and divine, both of which, as conceived here, entail personhood.

Let us begin by sketching four possible answers. (1) A man named Jesus of Nazareth. This is doubtless the most likely, perhaps the only likely answer to the question. A failed revolutionary, a blasphemer against the Jewish religion, a leader of a movement dangerous to the social orders of the day, both Jewish and Roman, a charismatic speaker who was capable of performing extraordinary (some would say miraculous) works primarily of healing, the man Jesus was executed by the authorities. We know the rest of this remarkable story. The Christian community, the proselytizers like the Apostle Paul, the rapid spread of a series of tenets of belief including a code of conduct and ritual observances, the establishment of a religion and a church follow. The explosion of documentary evidence a few centuries later provides details of the life and teachings of Jesus.

The death of the man Jesus per se is not what interests us. What followed from that death, its interpretation, is of enormous interest to anyone who cares about mankind, who has more than a passing interest in human behavior, understanding, and knowledge. The old religion of Judaism is expropriated by the followers of Jesus and transformed into a church. The church predictably develops a social, economic, and political order: leaders are appointed, helpers are enlisted, traitors are expelled and perhaps even killed. The consciousness of the Western mind is transformed and permanently reordered. That having been said, I must add that this first answer is indisputably the least interesting of the four, although this answer provides foundation for the fourth.

(2) Jesus Christ died on the cross, a being with a dual nature, both God and man. How Jesus Christ came to be in the first place is a matter of consummate mystery. I have argued in Chapter 4 that the Incarnation is nonsense, a paradigmatic confusion of time with eternity. What if Jesus died on the cross, but Christ or God lived on? Augustine asserts: "For when he took the form of a servant he did not lose the form of God" (*De trinitate* II.1.2, 98). This is mainline Christian doctrine, although it was disputed within the early church. Thus just as we may have granted the postulate at the beginning and its corollary, the Incarnation, so also may we grant the living God, in this case, Christ.

As Jesus Christ, God lived as the dual-natured being. Augustine comments:

> If we refer grace to knowledge and truth to wisdom, I think we shall not be inconsistent with the distinction between these two things which we have been recommending. Among things that have arisen in time the supreme grace is that man has been joined to God to form one person; among eternal things the supreme truth is rightly attributed to the Word of God. (*De trinitate* XIII.19.24, 367)

And at the moment of Jesus' death, God continued to live. God did not die on the cross. Only the human nature of Jesus Christ died on the cross.

What an outrage! God is a freeloader, riding around ancient Palestine in the body of Jesus of Nazareth, empowering him to perform various miraculous signs. But at the moment of death, when the wage of sin must be paid, God hops off. Jesus the man died for our sins. Jesus the man is left to his own loneliness, to suffer abandonment and estrangement, to lament being forsaken, as the abandoned sinner "to be sin" and to face meaninglessness on his own. The Son of God did not truly become man, for had he done so, he would have died on the cross along with the man Jesus.

This second answer is explicitly rejected by Paul, who writes: "For our sake [God] made [Christ] to be sin who knew no sin, so that in him we might become the righteousness of God" (2 Cor. 5:21). Here I entertain the possibility of separating that which Paul keeps joined.

(3) Jesus Christ died on the cross, a being with a dual nature, both God and man. This looks like the second answer, but in this case we consider that both Jesus and Christ died, as Paul claims. The dual natures, but one person, fully suffered death. For the story of redemption and salvation, this appears to be a better answer. In all four of our answers, I shall have Jesus the man die, but in this third answer God dies too. God is dead. Specifically, the Son of God has died. As difficult as it may be to conceive of God dying, we have in a way committed ourselves to it by granting the postulate and its corollary, the Incarnation. Life entails death. God lives, and so God must die. And in fact we can conceive of God dying by thinking of God as a person, a being among other beings.

We need not stand aghast at the prospect of a freeloading Christ. The story about the ultimate substitute sacrifice, the perfect paschal lamb, can continue. The especially abhorrent, Canaanite practice forbidden by the LORD to Israel, the sacrifice of the first-born male human being, has been undertaken by God himself.

Thus far one might be inclined to favor our third answer over the first two. Mankind is redeemed. But what are we to think about God? He is dead. Although I am about to write foolishness, I shall not engage in this particular bit of foolishness, i.e., to claim that God is also alive. No, God, the Son of God to be precise, has died on the cross. He died about 2,000 years ago. But God the Father is eternal, outside of time, undead to say the least. God is both dead and undead. I take care not to claim that God is simultaneously dead and undead, or to claim that God is dead and alive. That is not the third answer. The God who lived has died. For a brief period of thirty-three years, two thousand years ago, there was a living God, but not anymore. Of course, the God who is outside of time is God. God is dead and undead, but not at the same time. God is dead in time, starting from that Friday afternoon, but God is not undead in time. When we say "God is," or "God is undead," we do not really mean that God is undead now. God in the present is no different from God in the past or God in the future.

I do not assert that God has no relationship to time. God is the creator of time, provided that God is not bound by time, as I have assumed all along. (In the creative sense, time is not viewed as suffering, an imposition.) This creation is what so rightly baffles Augustine. We might say that God is the beginning of time (see the first chapter of John), and God is the end of time. But that is so in the way that the beginning of time is not in the past nor the end of time in the future. Nevertheless, at the end of the day, that Friday long ago, were we to take a divine census, we would come up with two Gods, one dead and one not dead, i.e., eternal.

(4) Jesus Christ died on the cross, a being with a dual nature, both God and man. This fourth answer looks like both the second and third answers, but here I draw the following distinctions. As with the first three answers, Jesus the man died. As with the third answer, God died. But with this fourth answer let us exact what might be considered the ultimate price for granting the nonsense of the Incarnation. God, not just a member of the family, is dead, God himself. God became man. God lived. Life entails death. God died. God entered time, and thus He lives no more, except perhaps metaphorically. This is the basis for the death of God movement in theology. Although the expression is associated with Hegel and Nietzsche, a group of writers in the 1960s, most notably Thomas Altizer, developed an interpretation of the expression. In his late writings, Bonhoeffer presented a position that is not quite as extreme as that of Altizer et al. While not claiming the death of God, Bonhoeffer writes that "God lets himself be pushed out of the world on to the cross. He is weak and powerless in the world, and that is precisely the way, the only way, in which he is with us and helps us" (*Letters from Prison* 360). Bonhoeffer seems to have traded the cross, a symbol of victory over death, for the crucifix that reveals God's love and Christ's suffering for mankind. It is as if Bonhoeffer has moved theologically from the inside of a Protestant church to the inside of a Catholic church.

According to Altizer (*New Gospel of Christian Atheism*), it was not until the nineteenth century, in particular with the writings of Hegel and Blake, that we were able to begin to understand the significance of the Crucifixion. Hegel's notion of *kenosis* describes what occurs on the cross. Blake and Hegel understood the "absolute self-emptying" to stand at the center of historical consciousness (Altizer, *Christian Atheism* 52). For Hegel this is "Spirit emptied out into Time ... externalization" (*Phenomenology* 808). Thus God emptied Himself out on the cross; He negated Himself absolutely; He died. This notion of *kenosis* is an extension of Paul's assertion regarding Jesus Christ, "who, though he was in the form of God, did not count equality with God a thing to be grasped, but emptied himself, taking the form of a servant (δοῦλος), being born in the likeness of men" (Phil. 2:6-7). He accepted time (Augustine). But such a notion is also discordant with Paul's claim that our Lord Jesus Christ is he "who alone has immortality and dwells in unapproachable light, whom no man has ever seen or can see" (1 Tim. 6:16).

Although all four of the answers deserve much more comment, I am merely laying out a sketch here. Before moving on to the implications of these answers, to the significance of the Resurrection, I will add a comment on the Incarnation.

Aquinas argues that Jesus Christ is one being, a single hypostasis or substance, with two natures. Divine nature can be predicated of him both in the abstract and in the concrete in that he is God. Human nature, however, can only be predicated of Christ in the concrete. Christ per se is not human nature (*Summa theologica* III.Q.17.A.1). "If both the natures were predicated in the abstract of Christ, it would follow that Christ is two" (*Summa theologica* III.Q.17.A.1). Aquinas notes further that, because Christ has a dual nature, things predicated to nature in Christ must be dual, whereas those things attributed to Christ alone must be single (*Summa theologica* III.Q.17.A.2). Thus, according to Augustine, we know Jesus Christ in two ways, according to contemplation and according to knowledge:

But all these things that the Word made flesh did and suffered for us in time and space belong ... to knowledge and not to wisdom. Insofar as he is the Word, he is without time and without space, coeternal with the Father and wholly present everywhere; and if anyone can utter a true word about this, as far as he is able, it will be a word of wisdom. So it is that the Word made flesh, which is Christ Jesus, has treasures both of wisdom and of knowledge. (*De trinitate* XIII.19.24, 366)

Since human nature entails life and death, we conclude that according to his human nature Jesus Christ died on the cross. But since divine nature is eternal, we also conclude that according to his divine nature death has no meaning. Death is temporal, whereas in his divinity Christ is eternal. According to Aquinas and traditional Christian theology, Jesus Christ is hypostatically one, God-man in the concrete.

When we consider in a taxonomic vein various answers to our question about the cross, we are viewing the matter from at least two perspectives, i.e., according to the nature of the thing—if that is at all possible—and according to its particularity. At each point where we are confounded, the confusion arises from mixing the temporal with the eternal. We are capable of holding the two perspectives just as we are capable of different kinds of knowing, one temporal and one not. As long as we restrict our consideration to the nature of the thing, or in the case of the Incarnation the natures of the thing, then we can keep separate the temporal from the eternal. It is in the particularity of the thing, the hypostasis of Jesus Christ, that we founder. Let us move now to the Resurrection.

* * *

If we take the first answer, the only answer that does not in a way insult our intelligence, then we must conclude that the Resurrection was a hoax. The dead man Jesus did not rise from the dead. If Jesus reappeared after the Crucifixion, as reported in the gospels, then he did not die on the cross. If he died on the cross, then he did not subsequently appear to his disciples. This position requires us to reject at least some portion of nearly every book in the New Testament, for there we are told explicitly that Jesus died and rose again.

One can easily think of reasons why Jesus and his disciples would want to conceal the fact that he did not die on that Friday. And just as easily, one can think of reasons why the disciples would want to fabricate the Resurrection of Jesus. The psychologist, the historian, the student of human behavior can give us numerous accounts. The Resurrection, the hoax, still interests us for what follows from it, for what we learn about ourselves. Solely in the history of ideas, the fabricated Resurrection commands our attention and respect, for it signals the wonderful manifestation of our thinking and of our spirit. The Resurrection becomes testimony to our affirmation of life, to our deep-seated hope, and to the power of our memory.

Our second answer gave us a freeloading Christ. To be more precise, the divinity of Jesus Christ did not die on the cross. But, of course, neither did the humanity of Jesus die. Jesus the individual and particular man died. If we are to accept the individualization of God as the Son of God made man, then we must take a position regarding this individual on that Friday afternoon. In this case we have divided the individual into two at the moment of death, resulting in a dead man and a living or at least undead God. In the story of redemption, we must seek anew the sacrifice.

Rather than the Crucifixion, the Incarnation then becomes the sacrifice, the ultimate suffering. Certainly, from a consideration of the two states, i.e., from the eternal and the temporal, the passage is infinite. The supreme act of love, resulting in the expiation of man's sin, now consists of a lowly birth. We have here what we may call an ironic God. In the story of redemption, we can dispense with the Crucifixion entirely. The significance of God's love is the birth of a child, not the execution of a blasphemous rebel. The Bible tells of a hidden God, but now we have the possibility of a completely hidden God, unrevealed.

Jesus the man is brought back from the dead, and is rejoined in life to his divinity. We are committed by the corollary of the Incarnation to a living God, and so in some way the divine Christ lived through the dark hours from Friday afternoon until Sunday morning. Under this interpretation, the preaching of Paul amounts to hot air, and is seriously misdirected. (Some have always argued this.) For Paul claims, "we preach Christ crucified, a stumbling block to Jews and folly to Gentiles" (1 Cor. 1:23). The Resurrection, at least from a human perspective, has been rendered into comedy by this second answer.

The third answer maintains the hypostatic integrity of Jesus Christ, one particular individual with two natures: human and divine. The individual in his totality died on the cross. Here we have a sign of God's love that is much more obvious than a lowly birth. God's love is manifest, it is revealed. The magnitude of Christ's suffering is no greater in this third case than in the second, because the suffering of the Incarnation is infinite. With this third answer we have added a finite, albeit truly horrible, amount of suffering. The magnitude remains the same, but the scandal is greatly magnified. The talk of kingdom now seems ironic. The folly is resplendent.

The resurrected Christ now signals a rebirth. Not only is the man Jesus returned to life, but also the Son of God, the living God, has been transformed. God truly became man, became living, and accordingly truly died. In regaining life, we are given an image of the kingdom, the heavenly reward, eternal life. The final enemy, death, has been defeated. Recall that this entire inquiry into faith and works has been initiated largely by Jesus' definition of eternal life (Jn 17:3). Although I have emphasized the eternal part in our study, here our attention is directed to life eternal.

I note the particularity of the entire redemption story. The creator did not become the creation, an idea or concept. God did not become mankind, another idea or concept. Nor did God become the incommensurability of the side with the diagonal of a square, an eternal truth or being according to Aristotle. Rather, the creator became a creature. God became man, one of us. He became temporalized. In so doing, in becoming Jesus of Nazareth, God suffered the particularity of being just one. In so doing, He died a particular, actual death. In its gruesome particularity, the death served as a sign to mankind that "once for all ... he offered up himself" (Heb. 7:27). Thus we become one in Christ, by which I do not mean brothers and sisters with Christ. By "one in Christ" I do not mean that God joined the human race, became a creature, one of us. I mean that the Son of God as Jesus Christ is one, an individual, as is each of us.

In comparison with the first two scenarios or answers, this one presents a relationship between object of belief and believer, between Jesus Christ and follower that differs significantly. In the first case the follower sees himself, perhaps magnified, in his leader, but his belief does not let him extend his thinking beyond himself. He is truly a brother with the slain Jesus of Nazareth, but the greatness of the leader entails no expansion or transformation of kind. The second case does not differ significantly from the first. The follower admires and perhaps envies Jesus the receptacle, the embodiment of the Son of God, as one would admire and envy another human being with appealing characteristics—good looks, bright mind, genial disposition. But the follower also sees himself in the dead man. The dead Jesus is honored, being raised from the dead and reunited with the Son of God, and so might we all be raised and honored one day.

With the third case, however, the relationship of the believer to the object truly is expanded. The disciple again is a brother of sorts with Jesus Christ in that they both share a nature, my previous comments notwithstanding. The disciple and Jesus Christ share human nature so fully that each, as a particular, faces death. But in this case the Son of God dies, too. The fear of abandonment and loneliness, the burden under which the follower lives his life, is experienced by the individual Jesus Christ, God and man. God is not lowered by his death. That occurred with the Incarnation. Jesus Christ is risen. The Son of God lives, and he who believes in him is transformed and made anew. Unlike beauty, reason, or the world, the believer's God is a personal God, and he himself is reflected in the risen Christ. He becomes god-like; he is remade in the image and likeness of God. We have Paul's new man.

With the fourth answer I ask: If God fully and totally emptied himself into the world, if the creator irrevocably became a creature in the Incarnation, then who or what rose from the dead? Altizer sees a new man (not Paul's), or more precisely a new mankind, "a Jesus who is present in every voice and face, and most immediately present in our deepest suffering and joy" (*Christian Atheism* 44).

We find in Bonhoeffer's later writings a version of this interpretation in which God does not disappear completely from the scene, but where the Christian is intently focused on this world. Only when one loves earthly life extremely may one believe in the Resurrection (*Letters from Prison* 157). "I should like to speak of God not on the boundaries but at the centre" (*Letters from Prison* 282). Accordingly, Augustine's knowledge and wisdom would converge onto one another.

This fourth answer, however, is more extreme than Bonhoeffer's position. It differs from the first answer in that here God really dies, whereas in the first answer God only figures into the argument in his absence. Somehow God abdicates his eternity by means of Incarnation and Crucifixion.

What has happened to the person-God if the risen Lord has become universal humanity? His personhood has become diffuse, spreading itself out into all mankind. What started out as the Son of God at the Incarnation has become God in every respect by the time of the Crucifixion. The investigation of previous answers included discussion of two natures, divine and human. With this fourth answer, the concern over natures is resolved historically. Divine and human nature have been fused together. With the Resurrection, the transformation has been completed. Man has been remade in the image and likeness of God to the point of eradicating the original. The original bled to death on the cross, and his godliness has been further bled out into all mankind.

And what about our person of faith, neither the believer in Hegelian dialectic nor the secularist, but the one who probably prefers the second or third answer? He is no better off than Augustine and Calvin. He stands before us along with his résumé that brims over with instances of hypocrisy and idolatry. He aspires to behold the beatific vision, and he intends to "go and not sin again," to pursue eternal life faithfully, expectant of grace. But when he reflects on the momentary character of his faithfulness, he is filled with fear and trembling, with anxiety. Tomorrow he may go to church or give to the poor, as he waits in pursuit, as he suffers time in pursuit of the eternal, as he waits hellishly for more grace. His sins may be totally forgiven, and the expiation of his sins may have been effected by an injection of the eternal into the temporal. In reversing the process, however, in grasping the eternal if only for a moment, he is haunted by his past and his future. Is it any wonder that the path out of this quandary seems to be in the direction of special atheism?

THE CANAANITE WOMAN

I turn to an incident reported by Matthew and Mark that may cause us to reconsider, or at least to re-evaluate our answers to the question: "Who died on the cross?" With respect to the being of Jesus Christ, i.e., who he is, his encounter with the Canaanite woman as reported by Matthew (15:21-8) is instructive. The passage is famous, perhaps infamous, and maybe even scandalous for the pious disciple of Christ. Jesus has gone down to Sidon and Tyre from Gennesaret when the woman calls to him. "Have mercy on me, O Lord, Son of David; my daughter is severely possessed by a demon." The woman is in need. Jesus ignores her. His disciples beg Jesus to "Send her away, for she is crying after us." Indirectly acknowledging the woman's existence, Jesus responds: "I was sent only to the lost sheep of the house of Israel." She persists: "Lord, help me." Jesus answers with a remark both caustic and demeaning. "It is not fair to take the children's bread and throw it to the dogs." She in turn replies: "Yes, Lord, yet even the dogs eat the crumbs that fall from their masters' table." Jesus extols the woman's faith and grants her wish. Her daughter is healed. We observe not only the woman's faith but also her resolve and quick wit. "Call me a dog? OK, then why don't you at least treat me like a dog?"

I consider this passage, however, not to marvel at the woman's mettle but rather to wonder what Jesus learned in the encounter. We know explicitly that Jesus was astonished by the woman's faith, faith in him to enlist the power of his father. How did Jesus feel? Was he shamed and humbled by her persistence? Did he confront and acknowledge his prejudice? After ignoring her initially, he called her a dog, presumably solely because she was a Canaanite. We do not receive answers to these questions. Jesus simply moves on after the encounter, and we are left to wonder. Who does Jesus think he is?

In the context of answers to "Who died on the Cross?" this passage fits most comfortably with the first answer. Jesus of Nazareth, a man, died on the cross. All men are prejudicial. Each of us is shamed and humbled, at least to some degree, by our own lack of consideration and kindness. "None is righteous, no, not one" (Rom. 3:10). It is unlikely, however, that Paul intends to include Jesus in this general condemnation. But do we see here a busy leader, preoccupied and harried, who was inconsiderate and negligent? Do we see the Teacher being taken to school?

At moments like these, the Face-of-Christ argument seems to be strongest, i.e., when we encounter Jesus the bigot, angry Jesus, or Jesus in despair. At exactly these moments, the Face overwhelms the Christ. Jesus is our brother. In him we recognize our genetic constitution, our kin. But what if Jesus is the Christ, the son of God, the true messiah? Are we witness here to the messiah in training, Jesus learning to show respect for each and every individual (not just the lost sheep of Israel) as he encounters the enormous faith embodied in this individual, the Canaanite woman?

Aquinas argues that Jesus Christ constitutes a single substance or hypostasis, but that this integral being has two natures, divine and human. We human beings read stories. Stories unfold in time and are bound by time. We too are bound by time. Thus we read the story of the life of Jesus, and we see, i.e., we come to know the man who prejudged the Canaanite woman, who earlier was rude to his mother (Lk. 2:48-9, Mt. 12:48-50) and who later despaired on the cross (Mt. 27:46). Even when we encounter the Word who is God, be that encounter through his preaching, his miracles, or his Resurrection, we do so necessarily through the filter of time, just as his preaching and miracles and Resurrection occurred in time.

In each of the four answers to the original question of this section, even the second with a freeloading Christ, we have Jesus the man, Jesus in time. We presume that as an infant, and then as a boy, as a teenager, as a young man, Jesus learned to function as a human being at an age-appropriate level. When did he learn to walk, to talk, to work at carpentry? These questions are mundane instances of the scandalous one asked here: When did Jesus learn that he was a bigot? No doubt he learned much from his parents, from others around him, and perhaps from the Canaanite woman.

What were his thoughts, his interior dialogue when he was 7 years old? At what age should he have begun to act like the Christ? We know that by age 12 Jesus had become a prodigy, one apparently on a mission. At that age he accompanied his parents to Jerusalem for Passover, but remained there when his parents left to return to Nazareth. His distraught parents eventually found him conversing with the teachers in the temple (Lk. 2:47). To his mother's rebuking question, he answered: "How is it that you sought me? Did you not know that I must be in my Father's house?" (Lk. 2:49). Luke concludes this passage: "And Jesus increased in wisdom and in stature, and in favor with God and man" (Lk. 2:52).

My aim here, bold and futile though it may be, is to demand of Jesus Christ that he be a man, and as such, to fall under the universal human injunction: Know thyself! The injunction itself may demand the impossible, to reify the temporal. As transcendent Christ, the only knowledge that Jesus Christ can have of himself, it would seem, is that as Christ he is transcendent. As we stand by and watch, surely we can hope for no more. Indeed, our knowledge comes from faith, and thus from our side it is more like firm opinion.

We are left to wonder what Jesus learned from his encounter with the woman who had so great a faith in him, or in the father through him. But this passage need not be merely a stumbling block for us who want to know who died on the cross. We learn that our temporal limitation, the temporality of faith, is one with Jesus Christ. We learn that if Jesus Christ has integrity, if we adopt the third answer to the original question, then that integrity, that single hypostasis, entails learning on the part of the Word. The learning, of course, may merely appear to us to be learning. By analogy it must also be learning for the integral Jesus Christ, but only by analogy. To claim more would be to undo the paradox. In so doing we would confuse the temporal with the eternal, as we have done, do, and shall do many more times. If the temporal and the eternal are fused in the single hypostasis, we are condemned to confuse them.

13

Atheism and the Face of Christ

Throughout this study, I have argued that complete and total atheism is impossible. We all kneel before the altar of some god or another. Most of us are polytheists. This is so quite simply because we are creatures of faith. We desire the condition of faith, its attendant anxiety notwithstanding. Do we also desire the anxiety? For Paul Tillich, atheism amounts to claiming to be unconcerned about the meaning of one's existence (*Dynamics of Faith* 52). Most so-called atheists, therefore, deny belief in the person-God, and in particular belief in the God of Abraham, especially as interpreted by the Apostle Paul (Special Atheism). For them, this God is not.

Although there is no absolute atheism, it is easy to trace a secularization of faith, an unfolding in the world of a religious sentiment that shifts significantly the emphasis from a transcendent, eternal being or presence to a collective rooted in the world. The fourth answer to our question regarding "Who died on the cross?," God, in every sense, has increasingly taken root in our consciousness.

Bonhoeffer foresees a religion-less Christianity. Thomas Altizer proclaims Christian atheism. There is also ample evidence for religious practice accompanying special atheism: Sunday assemblies, sacred meals, locations designated for meditation and unspecified worship. I offer the following example of how seemingly well-intentioned Christian sentiment and thought can lead to the slow but certain ebbing away of God, how every last drop of divinity can be drained out of Jesus Christ, how God could have bled to death on the cross.

Then the righteous will answer him, "Lord, when did we see thee hungry and feed thee, or thirsty and give thee drink? … " And the King will answer them, "Truly, I say to you, as you did it to one of the least of these my brethren, you did it to me." (Mt. 25:37-40)

This passage is frequently cited to support the notion that Jesus Christ is among us in those whom we encounter daily. According to Christian doctrine, Jesus Christ is man, and in that sense Christians can rightly call him brother, a fellow human being. Reciprocally, just as Christ is in the hungry, the thirsty, the stranger, he must also be in each one of us.

The Second Commandment forbids man from forming images of God. God remains hidden. Augustine asserts: "Now divinity cannot be seen by human sight in any way whatever" (*De trinitate* I.6.11, 74). Paul claims that our Lord Jesus Christ "alone has immortality and dwells in unapproachable light, whom no man has ever seen or can see" (1 Tim. 6:16). But man does know Jesus Christ, even if only as Jesus of Nazareth. Through revelation, by means of signs, man is made aware of Jesus Christ, the unbegotten son of God. Thus man thinks that he has discovered God, in particular God in man. Hegel would go so far as to claim that only in man is God found: "For example, the Christian imagination will be able to represent God in human form and its expression of *spirit*, only because God himself is here completely known in himself as *spirit*" (*Aesthetics* 75). "[F]or God to be spirit he must appear as man, as an individual subject—not as ideal humanity, but as actual progress into the temporal and complete externality of immediate and natural existence" (*Aesthetics* 435). God apparently is disclosed, the veil of hiding is removed. Man forms an image of God and thus man comes to know God in Jesus Christ, but he knows God only as a man. This is the man of spirit, but the spirit is inferred from the actions of men and from our own consciousness. We imbue the image with the imageless.

The notion that Christ is in us and we in him is expanded such that creation can be considered a medium. When a creature praises God, it is God praising God through the medium of creation. Augustine writes: "It is a yet further matter to say that when a man sees something which is good, God in him sees that it is good. That is, God is loved in that which he has made, and he is not loved except through the Spirit which he has given" (*Confessions* XIII. xxxi.46). Conversely, when a creature loves the creator it loves all creation (1 Jn 5:1-2). We creatures can appreciate the humanity of Jesus Christ, and accordingly can take seriously his temptation by the devil, his feeling of abandonment on the cross, and even his prejudicial treatment of the Canaanite woman and his chastising response to his mother. The creatures, referring to themselves, can appreciate further the spirit of Jesus Christ, which may be necessary to comprehend the actions of the devil as temptations. But beyond this, the creatures need revelation.

Thus we might see the face of Christ in those around us if we make an effort to see him. Such counsel provides illumination and guidance to various Christian charities. The service performed by the members of the charitable organizations is directed ultimately to Christ. God in man, not man in God. The world is full of Christians attempting to live Christ-like lives.

God in one person sees God in another. This effort to see the face of Christ is a step toward the total humanizing of the Son of God. The face of Christ has a tendency to backfire. Rather than seeing Jesus Christ in our fellow man, we see our fellow man in Jesus Christ. The notion or blade is double-edged, cutting in both directions and doing damage both ways. By seeing Christ in our brother or sister, do we not run the risk of obscuring or categorizing the person? By turning the person into a representative, we strip him of individuality. But here I am developing only the damage caused in the other direction.

I noted in the third answer to "Who died on the cross?" the particularity and individuality of the Son of God become man. As individuals, Jesus Christ and each one of us face death, the consequence of sin. Each fears abandonment and loneliness. The disciple is reflected in the God-man and, through the resurrection of Jesus Christ, he acquires divinity.

Now we turn to our fellow human beings. Do we approach Christ in the hungry, the thirsty, the stranger, and by extrapolation in our neighbor? Do we encounter God in His creatures and come to know something about Him through them? Perhaps, but in this encounter do we not also debase the divinity? We do so not by ripping God from the heavens, but rather by diluting the deity, softening Him. Can the Christian help but humanize the Son of God? The rip did not occur at the Christian's behest. "God so loved the world." But it is one thing for God to humble himself, and it is quite another for us to humble God, effectively to enslave God.

The evangelist writes in human terms, as did Jesus speak of the father and the son. Accordingly, we bear the burden of love by humanizing it. If one is repelled by the notion of man making God in his own image and likeness, there is recourse to the fourth answer with its Hegelian roots of Spirit and its extension. God so thoroughly made man in His image that ultimately the images blended together.

God did not die because he was hidden. He did not waste away. He did not die from loneliness and neglect. God died when he was revealed completely to mankind, when he came out of the closet. A remarkable metamorphosis, as if a resplendent butterfly has been transformed into a caterpillar.

As noted in Chapter 12, answers (1) and (4) lead to special atheism. Here we have drained the mystery and miracle out of the God-man. We have repudiated the third answer. Perhaps it is the development of spirit in the world. We are then left with the ultimate version of "made in the image and likeness" of God. The divine exists in all men; indeed, the divine has no separate existence from mankind. God is man's best man.

14

Concluding Remarks

In Chapter 1 I acknowledged some of the limitations of this inquiry. Had I drawn on writings from outside the Western tradition, had I delved into so-called mystical works, the results certainly would differ from what I have produced. Had I subjected God to time, this study would not exist. Had I treated Jesus Christ solely as our brother, my attention would have been directed almost exclusively to our temporal being and world. (It is, in a sense, so directed no matter what one presupposes.) I have attempted, rather, to think about faith as the pursuit of knowledge, and to understand faith as actual, i.e., as a choking, temporal phenomenon that results in action owing to its inherently contradictory nature. Had my title been either "Steadfast Faith" or "Anxious Faith," the contents of the book would have been unchanged.

I presume that anyone who came to this study in search of the spark of faith or in the hopes of having his faith strengthened stopped reading long before reaching these concluding remarks. I presume further that nothing written here would shake one's "conviction in things not seen," although I have presented an interpretation of conviction (ἔλεγχος) that would more aptly render the word as testing. A sign is necessary for faith but hardly sufficient. The emphasis here has been on God as eternal action and on a transcendent Christ. But here at the end, these pages do not point unequivocally in one direction or another. They constitute neither an argument for the existence of God nor an exhortation to keep the faith. They are not an apology for faith but rather they stand in wonder of it.

Central to these considerations has been the postulate: "God is not bound by time." We exist temporally. That is what to exist means for us. In one respect, our temporality can be thought of as a suffering; we suffer time. But, in another respect, time is not an external imposition, a thing outside of us and applied to our being. It is part of who we are, especially who we are as sinners. It may seem odd to describe the organization of our being as sin, and I acknowledge the need for a fuller treatment of that description. But I have proposed and accepted the possibility that we encounter or uncover the timeless in logical consequence. Succession is not supported by time; time is supported by succession. And this succession is not of an arbitrary sort, but rather it is necessary. It is logical entailment. Accordingly, our organization is thrown into relief against a kind of organization that is truly authentic, our suffering in comparison to what of necessity must follow. With this understanding of consequence one is able to entertain the postulate and its implications. God, the creator, is eternal action. God created time. Thus there is time and there is not time. In response to Augustine's joking but serious question "What was God doing before he created time?" I have offered an interpretation of before. I differ from Augustine in allowing for the indefinite extension of time both into the past and the future.

My concentration on Christianity has led me to consider the Incarnation as a corollary of the postulate. The Incarnation is a possibility, given that God is not bound by time. The eternal has been injected into the temporal in a unique way. The Son of God became man. Reciprocally we become one with Christ, a unity that we seek to understand as we bring together the eternal and the temporal. The eternal and the temporal intersect whenever a temporal being such as we contemplates the necessary. Such contemplation is hardly unique: the world is full of rational, sentient beings who touch the necessary. These are events, but the Incarnation is not one of them. The Incarnation is the unique event, the melding of all eternity with all temporality. It occurs in the fullness of time because it is, along with the Crucifixion and the Resurrection, the expiation of all sin, the transformation of time. "Yes, Lord ... you are the Christ who is coming into the world."

In principle, this study concerns faith in general, and I have given several examples of kinds of faith without developing any one but the Judeo-Christian faith. This latter faith may differ from many or all of the others in its object, which cannot correctly be called a being, since doing so implies that the object, God, belonged to the class of beings. We name the object God and in one sense can say little about it other than that God is that which is supremely. God is Being. On the one hand, we might even wish to remove the "ing" from God's being. The eternal God is not substance, standing under all that is, for in that sense God would not be eternal, but in fact temporal: stand-ing. On the other hand, let us say that God became man. God lives. Some would say that we blaspheme merely by uttering the name "God," although the Judeo-Christian faith draws us to God. Through revelation we also refer to God as "He."

The Christian faith, like all faith, has been shown to be inherently anxious. Consequently, works issue forth, but this issuance is not a temporal consequence, although worldly works are necessarily temporal, just as is faith. One does not believe today and act tomorrow. Faith and works are not separated by time. The anxiety that attends this conception of faith is evident in my investigation itself. The wonder of thought is no less evident in questions, even perhaps vexatious ones, than it is in praise and adoration. Even in my most obstinate and graceless moments, there may be a hint of grace shining though.

The person of faith seeks knowledge, and the Christian seeks to know God and Jesus Christ. When we read that the Christian seeks to be justified, I understand that he seeks to be right, he seeks to know and to understand. If he also seeks rest, it is rest in the truth, Augustine's Sabbath rest, contemplation of the beatific vision. This search is an eternal one, embarked upon in a temporal manner. Some might describe it as a quest to encounter Being. If religion is to be of any assistance, it will be so only in a temporal sense. Religion may help the believer keep the faith for a moment, and then for another moment. Religion will not eradicate the loneliness and estrangement of original sin, the anxiety; religion will not expiate sin or transform time, but it may provide a meeting place for the fellowship of abandoned sinners, a communion of hypocritical and idolatrous aliens, each staring meaninglessness in the face. Even if we confine our attention to true religion, i.e., the relationship between the Creator and creation, in so doing we find answers that really are restatements of the questions of faith. Each answer may be deeper, more profound than the question that elicited it, but each answer to the question of faith is a temporal response to an eternal question.

Our faith, an inherently contradictory undertaking, is constantly under attack, and we fallen and inauthentic human beings are the enemy. We are students of human nature, and as such we find ourselves to be victims. We view time as an external condition to which we are subject. Things happen to us. We find lipstick on the collar and our faith is shaken. We thirst for signs, for assurance, both that the object of faith is the truth and that we ourselves are trustworthy. Accordingly, we test ourselves. But our studies, in one regard, have been too successful. We are well acquainted with the problems of good intentions among temporal beings. Temporal beings, beings per se, necessarily are buffeted. We shift allegiances. There appear to be world trends, one of which seems to be the gradual but inexorable disappearance of the transcendent God. God became man. The end.

Where does this leave us, the interested students of faith, other than weary? Fatigue is not a place of repose and certainly not the rest sought by Augustine, although in a way fatigue makes death more acceptable in a worldly sense. We wait. Regarding all the problems with time and eternity, the person of faith might say to himself that he will leave those matters to God to sort out. No choking. Such may be a prudent decision with regard to living a life of faith, to living at all. For the person of faith capitulation may be the only answer, because there exists no other answer. Nonetheless, I reject weariness and fatigue as a conclusion to my study, even if we all become worn down by life, even if each and every one of us dies exhausted. I refuse to let my investigation die as did Don Quixote, Alonso el Apostato, making out a will. I have attempted to remain resolutely quixotic. Better it would be perhaps for us to place our faith in the resurrection of humanity, an Easter of mankind. Better it would be to look back to the good Friday when God was nailed to the cross and see the new truth. Better it would be to appropriate the Incarnation and to understand it, to consider Jesus Christ to be the first among men. The transcendent, the eternal action ruptured time once for all, becoming temporalized. In so doing, time became the horizon of Being (Heidegger), and eternity died.

God bled out his divinity, *kenosis*, into the soil that formed the foundation for the cross. The divine blood seeped into the earth and fertilized it. From this most fecund humus a new man sprang up, un-Pauline. The new man grew up and blossomed. Spirit was in the world and only in the world.

There may be several endings to this inquiry. The one just now described is fanciful, with its agricultural rite of spring. Other endings will be no less fanciful. Even Don Quixote is not completely faithless. He has switched allegiances from knight errantry to the world, its customs and mores. One passion, mundane, dull, and common though it may be, replaced another.

There is, of course, an alternative to the postulate. Let us bind the hands of God with time. One consequence of this restriction might be the historical development and unfolding of Spirit in the world. Another consequence might be a Lucretian world of matter and force, or a Marxist world of social relations essentially derived from productive forces. These are subjects or paths for an inquiry different from this one, to be carried out by someone other than me.

I acknowledge the narrow scope of this study. Where in these pages is the feeling, the emotion that generates and supports faith? "Say 'Amen!' somebody." Can community and the support of other human beings be of so little significance as to receive scant mention here? Cannot we align our thinking with John, who sees our love of God through Jesus Christ as rebounding to encompass all who believe that Jesus is the Christ? We, the children, by loving the parent, love all of the other children. We express this love by obeying God's commandments, which are not burdensome (1 Jn 5:1-3). Is not faith also a way of life, filled with ritual? In that sense, faith is positive. Faith is hopeful. A path is prescribed for the follower. The believer need not anxiously wait. He need not pursue necessarily in vain because the objective, the goal, is unattainable. These considerations all seem to be parts of faith, and they are distinct from our faith as pursuit of knowledge. People who claim to be faithful, although they are hypocrites and idolaters, engage in these activities. The very wonder of faith is manifest in the resolve of the faithful, in the face of their hypocrisy, idolatry, and unfaithfulness, to confess anew, to keep the faith. In looking back over this inquiry, one might reasonably ask: "Where is such grace?"

Among many other possible directions, I find inviting and tempting the one that is indicated negatively by Bonhoeffer when he writes, "for a man whose only support is his conscience can never realize that a bad conscience may be stronger and more wholesome than a deluded one" (*Letters from Prison* 4). Loosely, I have referred to this course as prudent, indicating its temporal and contextual nature. And we can be certain that there are no good consciences.

But, in the face of faith, this temptation looks to be positively evil. Starbuck is a prudent man.

Some of my conclusions may seem bleak or disappointing, but in fact they are neither. We temporal beings favor one side. We admire the faithful person, e.g., the martyr, even when we do not share the same belief. More striking are professions of faith in the face of misfortune. The faithful person affirms his faith in the deity while suffering a calamity. In most cases, such affirmations are expressions of hope for a better day, if not in this world then in the next. But, on rare occasion, we might witness resolve to abide in faithfulness even without any hope of relief from misfortune. In literature we have Faulkner's Lucas Beauchamp and Melville's Ahab. And we often hear expressed by someone who lacks faith the wish or desire for a God who truly cares for us, and if not our omni-God, our eternal action, at least someone with clout. Perhaps a beneficent Zeus.

Our partiality, according to Kant, extends beyond our feeling. He claims that a rational being has an interest on the positive side of his antinomies, the fourth of which is: There is an absolutely necessary being. Kant writes, "reason's architectonic interest (which demands not empirical but pure a priori rational unity) carries with it a natural commendation for the assertions of the thesis" (*Critique of Pure Reason* B 503). Thus it should come as no surprise that the anxiety that attends the faith studied here differs little from the reason that "restlessly seeks the unconditionally necessary" (Kant, *Grounding* 62). These are the beings we are.

One might also have wished to read more about a creator, God, who has a personal interest in the individuals of his creation. The Bible repeatedly and expressly reveals this kind of God, a creator who so loved his creation that he sent his only son. What can one make of the eternal actor who takes an interest in the world? Is he a contradiction? Interest, care, and concern all seem to entail temporality. But, of course, the world itself entails temporality. The contradiction is epitomized by the Incarnation. The Word is God who is coming into the world. The changeless changes. According to Augustine, this is the intersection of wisdom and knowledge, truth and grace. According to Aquinas, the confusion comes about from the creature speaking about the creator in creaturely ways. Can it be that divine love is so great that it overwhelms and stuns the understanding? Is this our encounter with the Being of beings? Augustine would say "yes" and Heidegger would say "no."

At least part of the confusion arises from our conception of a person. We conceive of an object with attributes. A person, as object, may be tall or short, courageous or cowardly, generous or miserly. We conceive of the person independent of most or all of the attributes, a separate being to whom the attributes are attached. In so conceiving, we do not attribute both tall and short or both courageous and cowardly to the person, at least not at the same time and in the same way. Thus with God one may attribute to him both justice and mercy, although I readily acknowledge along with Anselm that these attributes as we understand them cannot be so in the same way, at least as we understand them.

The problem of attribution is exacerbated when we think of eternity, timelessness, as a characteristic of God, since eternity seems to be all encompassing. (We fare no better when we say with Augustine that God is in a sense the only being.) How can there be a time when God is eternal? But God is not a being who also is eternal. God does not possess a divine nature which is one among many natures. God is the eternal actor, pure act according to Aquinas. His care and concern for the individuals of his creation are of interest to us because care and concern are human, temporal traits. God is not a being who also cares for us.

More generally, I might be faulted for not saying much at all about God's being, although I have at least pointed to the problem. I have adopted or modified Augustine's sense of supreme being. Let God be that which is supremely. Ultimately, I refuse to consider God as a being among many other beings, such as Jesus of Nazareth, the number seven, or the incommensurability of the side and diagonal of a square. And yet we refer to God as He.

I have attempted to take seriously the opening verses of the Gospel of John. "In the beginning was the Word, and the Word was with God, and the Word was God" (Jn 1:1-3). In short, I have pursued the notion that Jesus Christ is God and not merely the first among men. Faith is the pursuit of the knowledge of God and of Jesus Christ (Jn 17:3), the Being of beings. Being. Coupled with the postulate, this pursuit has led to contradiction. A pastoral response here might be: embrace the paradox! If by embrace one means live with it, then there seems to be no alternative. I suspect that at times by embrace one means ignore. I attempt to persevere in my inquiry about the transcendent Jesus Christ. "My mind is on fire (*exarsit*) to solve this very intricate enigma" (Augustine, *Confessions*

XI.xxii.28). Some other possibilities—Jesus was a man, or God truly died on the cross—have at times appeared to be better paths or at least paths more easily followed.

Heidegger asks: "*Why* does this reifying keep coming back to exercise its dominion?" (*Being and Time* H437). The caution is apt. Our language leads us to make things, in English, by adding "-tion" to verbs. Are these things: extinction, inception, incarnation? One must also beware of gerunds. Reifying turns *be* into *being*, the ultimate gerund. I balk at the thing-hood of time, claiming that it does not exist while acknowledging that time is and is not. Heidegger sees this as temptation by belief in the eternal.

I equate reifying with Augustine's rest. But reifying is active and centered on man. The desire to know is a human characteristic. My entire study of faith has revolved around this desire. The human quest is one that searches for things, in particular, the truth. Both desire and reifying as actions are temporal. The word "rest" itself connotes temporality. But Augustine's rest is not in time. This rest is knowledge, contemplation, the true objective of faith. It constitutes an end to Calvin's perpetual struggle that is faith. Where Heidegger sees temptation, Augustine sees fulfillment.

With Augustine, one may desire rest, and further one may attempt to attain it, to seek it by means of faith. But one will not find rest in faith per se. Quite the opposite. In faith one may discover life, albeit a life filled with anxiety and contradiction. Surely he was a great ironist who said "my yoke is easy and my burden is light." He was responding to another great ironist who commanded: Know thyself! Lord, grant me the grace not to live a life of irony.

15

The Coroner of Jerusalem

I imagine someone who lived at the time of Jesus of Nazareth, and who had an official position in the city of Jerusalem, that of coroner. This man may have been a Jew, but not necessarily. Regardless of his ethnic and religious background, he could serve as official coroner for the city only with the sanction of the local Roman leaders. I imagine further that the coroner was on the job on that Friday afternoon when Jesus of Nazareth was crucified, apparently along with some other criminals, and that as part of his official duties as coroner he was to verify the deaths of those persons condemned to be executed.

Late in the afternoon on that day, he was called to inspect the body of the criminal Jesus, which he did, and to verify that Jesus was indeed dead, which indeed he was. There may have been some haste with the impending Sabbath beginning at sundown, but the coroner was at his post. He was experienced in these matters, crucifixions being fairly regular occurrences in those days, even on Fridays. If anyone on the entire face of the earth could be certain that Jesus had died, it would be the coroner. He was the judge, the local arbiter of death. Thus he could say with certainty that Jesus had died. I suppose further, maybe for no special reason, that he accompanied the group of mourners, Joseph of Arimathea and the women who had come from Galilee, to the rock-hewn tomb where the body of Jesus was laid. And for good measure, the coroner witnessed the sealing of the tomb's opening with a boulder.

The following day was the Sabbath. On Sunday the coroner arose early, very early, before sunrise. Why he awoke and got up so early is of little matter. Whether he had slept well or poorly on Saturday night, whether he awoke in a tranquil or agitated mood does not matter. For some reason, on Sunday, early in the morning the coroner got up, left his dwelling, and went for a walk. Whether or not he planned his itinerary I do not know. Perhaps his mind was occupied with other matters, for example, the week that lay before him at work, and his feet, so to speak, walked where they wanted to walk. This is not to claim that the coroner knew nothing about Jesus, the man crucified last Friday. That would be inconceivable. Even the most preoccupied functionary in the Roman-Jewish establishment could not have been so isolated as not to have heard about the crowds, the alleged miracles, the claims about kingdom and kingship. The executed man was notorious, at least locally. Notorious, but hardly unique. There were lots of criminals, some almost unknown, others, like that Barabbas fellow, virtual celebrities.

So the coroner may have slept well on Saturday night, and the night before too, because the weekend's events were not extraordinary. On the other hand, he may have tossed and turned all night, as he may have the night before, thinking about the crucifixion of Jesus. Maybe the coroner was even a clandestine disciple of Jesus, having heard much about his preaching and his miraculous works. The coroner himself may have heard Jesus speak on occasion, although if so he was circumspect, careful not to be identified as a follower of Jesus. In any event, on that early Sunday morning the feet of the coroner led him to the vicinity of the tomb where the body of Jesus had been placed. Perhaps he did not realize where he was, although he was aware that the sun was about to rise. It was a cloudless morning, quite unlike the previous Friday afternoon.

At daybreak, while the coroner was passing the tomb, the boulder rolled away and Jesus walked out. It is not important what other events may have occurred in that place at that time. Perhaps there was an earthquake. Perhaps the coroner heard trumpet blasts come from the heavens. I can imagine that he may have seen in the distance people running toward the tomb, Mary Magdalene, Mary the mother of James, Salome, and Simon Peter, but they had not yet arrived. But perhaps, except for the chirping of birds, there were no sounds. The earth was still and solid beneath his feet. There was no one around except for Jesus and himself. No angel.

I do not know nor particularly care if Jesus spoke to the coroner. The boulder having been rolled away, Jesus may have simply exited the tomb and walked off. On the other hand, he may have turned toward the coroner and smiled. Approaching him, Jesus may have placed his hand on the coroner's shoulder, embraced him, or even given him a kiss. None of this matters, but what happened next does. I shall consider two possibilities.

Upon seeing this remarkable event, the coroner may have exclaimed: "My Lord and my God!" It has been determined that he knew or had heard, at the very least, something about the crucified man, the man who cured lepers of their sores, enabled the lame to walk again, and brought the dead back to life. This was the man who had spoken about kingdom, a politically charged term that reverberated throughout Jewish and Roman circles alike. This was the man who promised his followers eternal life, whatever that was.

Now the coroner has witnessed the resurrection of Jesus from the dead. In response he has shown himself to be a plagiarist in anticipation, quoting the famous exclamation, yet to be uttered, by Doubting Thomas. Recall that Thomas will be confronted by the risen Jesus, who will insist that Thomas touch his wounds in order to verify what Thomas sees, and to shame him. Regarding that famous exclamation, many commentators, from Augustine to Dostoevsky, have observed that Thomas saw, i.e., knew one thing and believed another. He knew what he saw and touched, the risen Jesus. He believed that he was in the presence of his Lord and God.

And so too, perhaps, with the coroner, who may in fact have been a disciple all along. Even if he was not a follower of Jesus, he may have made the same exclamation. It was true, all that he had heard about fair-skin lepers and dancing cripples. The signs pointed to the truth: Jesus was the Christ, the Messiah, the Son of God. On this Sunday morning, by means of a most remarkable sign—the rolling boulder, the walking man whom he had certified as dead the previous Friday—he believed that he was in the presence of his Lord and God. As an alternative, and instead of a profession of faith, my coroner may have asked: "How did he do that?"

BIBLIOGRAPHY

Altizer, Thomas J. J. *The New Gospel of Christian Atheism*. Aurora, Colorado: The Davies Group, 2002.

Anselm. *Proslogium* in *Saint Anselm. Basic Writings*. 2nd edn. Trans. S. N. Deane. La Salle, Illinois: Open Court, 1962.

Aquinas, St. Thomas. *Summa theologica. Christian Classics Ethereal Library*. http://www.ccel.org/ccel/aquinas/summa.html (accessed February 6, 2019).

Aristotle. *Aristotelis. Physica*. Ed. W. D. Ross. London: Oxford University Press, 1950.

Aristotle. *Physics*. Trans. R. P. Hardie and R. K. Gaye. *The Complete Works of Aristotle*. Vol. 1. Ed. Jonathan Barnes. Princeton, New Jersey: Princeton University Press, 1984.

Aristotle. *Aristotle's Physics: A Guided Study*. Trans. and annot. Joe Sachs. New Brunswick, New Jersey: Rutgers University Press, 1995.

Augustine. *The Confessions of Augustine*. Ed. John Gibb and William Montgomery. Cambridge: Cambridge University Press, 1927 [All Latin words in *Confessions* quotations are taken from this edition].

Augustine. *Confessions*. Trans. and annot. Henry Chadwick. Oxford: Oxford University Press, 1991 [All *Confessions* quotations in English are from this translation].

Augustine. *The Trinity* [*De trinitate*]. *The Works of Saint Augustine: A Translation for the 21st Century*. 2nd edn. Trans. and annot. Edmund Hill, O.P. Hyde Park, New York: New City Press, 1991.

Augustine. *The City of God against the Pagans*. Ed. and trans. R. W. Dyson. Cambridge: Cambridge University Press, 1998.

Augustine. *Enarrationes in psalmos*. "In psalmum 74. Enarratio. Sermo ad plebem." https://www.augustinus.it/latino/esposizioni_salmi/index2.htm (accessed February 6, 2019).

Augustine. *Homilies on the Gospel of John*. Trans. John Gibb. *Nicene and Post-Nicene Fathers*. First Series. Vol. 7. Ed. Philip Schaff. Rev. and ed. Kevin Knight. New Advent. http://www.newadvent.org/fathers/1701029.htm (accessed February 6, 2019).

Augustine. *On Christian Doctrine* [*De doctrina Christiana*]. Trans. James Shaw. *Nicene and Post-Nicene Fathers*. First Series. Vol. 2. Ed.

Philip Schaff. Rev. and ed. Kevin Knight. New Advent. http://www.newadvent.org/fathers/12022.htm (accessed February 6, 2019).

Augustine. *On the Gift of Perseverance* [*De dono perseverantiae*]. Trans. Peter Holmes and Robert Ernest Wallis. Rev. Benjamin B. Warfield. *Nicene and Post-Nicene Fathers*. First Series. Vol. 5. Ed. Philip Schaff. Rev. and ed. Kevin Knight. New Advent. http://www.newadvent.org/fathers/1512.htm (accessed February 6, 2019).

Augustine. *On the Grace of Christ, and On Original Sin* [*De gratia Christi, et de peccato originali*]. Trans. Peter Holmes and Robert Ernest Wallis. Rev. Benjamin B. Warfield. *Nicene and Post-Nicene Fathers*. First Series. Vol. 5. Ed. Philip Schaff. Rev. and ed. Kevin Knight. New Advent. http://www.newadvent.org/fathers/15061.htm (accessed February 6, 2019).

Augustine. *On the Predestination of the Saints* [*De praedestinatione sanctorum*]. Trans. Peter Holmes and Robert Ernest Wallis. Rev. Benjamin B. Warfield. *Nicene and Post-Nicene Fathers*. First Series. Vol. 5. Ed. Philip Schaff. Rev. and ed. Kevin Knight. New Advent. http://www.newadvent.org/fathers/1512.htm (accessed February 6, 2019).

Augustine. *On Rebuke and Grace* [*De correptione et gratia*]. Trans. Peter Holmes and Robert Ernest Wallis. Rev. Benjamin B. Warfield. *Nicene and Post-Nicene Fathers*. First Series. Vol. 5. Ed. Philip Schaff. Rev. and ed. Kevin Knight. New Advent. http://www.newadvent.org/fathers/1513.htm (accessed February 6, 2019).

Barth, Karl. *The Epistle to the Romans*. 1918. 6th edn. Trans. Edwyn C. Hoskyns. London: Oxford University Press, 1933.

Barth, Karl. "Die Menschlichkeit Gottes." *Theologische Studien*, 48, 1956.

Barth, Karl. "The Humanity of God." *The Humanity of God*. 1956. Trans. John Newton Thomas. Louisville, Kentucky: John Knox Press, 1960.

Beckett, Samuel. *Waiting for Godot: Tragicomedy in 2 Acts*. New York: Grove Press, 1954.

Bible. *The Greek New Testament*. 3rd edn. New York: American Bible Society, 1962.

Bible. *The New Oxford Annotated Bible with the Apocrypha*. RSV. Oxford: Oxford University Press, 1962.

Bonhoeffer, Dietrich. "The Cost of Discipleship." 1937. *Dietrich Bonhoeffer: Witness to Jesus Christ*. Ed. John de Gruchy. San Francisco: Collins, 1987.

Bonhoeffer, Dietrich. *The Cost of Discipleship*. 1937. Trans. R. H. Fuller and Irmgard Booth. New York: Simon & Schuster, 1995.

Bonhoeffer, Dietrich. *Letters & Papers from Prison: The Enlarged Edition*. 1953. Ed. Eberhard Bethge. Trans. Reginald Fuller and Frank Clark. New York: Simon & Schuster, 1997.

Buber, Martin. *Ich und Du.* Leipzig: Insel Verlag, 1923.

Buber, Martin. *Zwei Glaubensweisen.* Zürich: Manesse Verlag, 1950.

Buber, Martin. *I and Thou.* 1923. 2nd edn. Postscript by the Author. Trans. Ronald Gregor Smith. New York: Charles Scribner's Sons, 1958.

Buber, Martin. *Two Types of Faith.* 1950. Trans. Norman P. Goldhawk. London: Routledge & Kegan Paul, 2003.

Calvin, John. *Ioannia Calvini opera quae supersunt omnia.* Ed. Edouard Cunitz, Johann-Wilhelm Baum, Eduard Wilhelm Eugen Reuss. Braunschweig: C. A. Schwetschke and Filium, 1864.

Calvin, John. *Institutes of the Christian Religion.* 1536. Trans. Henry Beveridge. Peabody, Massachusetts: Hendrickson Publishers, 2008.

Cervantes Saavedra, Miguel de. *El Ingenioso Hidalgo Don Quijote de la Mancha.* 1605 and 1615. Ed. and annot. Tom Lathrop. Newark, Delaware: Juan de la Cuesta, 1997.

Cervantes Saavedra, Miguel de. *Don Quixote.* 1605 and 1615. Trans. Edith Grossman. Intro. Harold Bloom. New York: HarperCollins Publishers, 2003.

Dedekind, Richard. "The Nature and Meaning of Numbers." 1893. *Essays on the Theory of Numbers.* Trans. Wooster Woodruff Beman. New York: Dover Publications, 1963.

Dostoevsky, Fyodor. *The Brothers Karamazov.* 1879–1880. Trans. Richard Pevear and Larissa Volokhonsky. New York: Random House, 1990.

Eliot, George. *Middlemarch.* 1871–1872. Ed. W. J. Harvey. London: Penguin Group, 1965.

Euclid. *The Thirteen Books of Euclid's Elements.* 3 vols. Trans. and annot. Thomas L. Heath. 1908. New York: Dover Publications, 1956.

Faulkner, William. *Go Down, Moses.* 1940. New York: Vintage International, 1990.

Francis. The Supreme Pontiff Francis. *Lumen fidei.* 2013. http://w2.vatican.va/content/francesco/it/encyclicals/documents/papa-francesco_20130629_enciclica-lumen-fidei.html (accessed February 6, 2019).

Hegel, Georg Wilhelm Friedrich. *Aesthetics: Lectures on Fine Art.* 1835. Trans. T. M. Knox. 2 vols. Oxford: Oxford University Press, 1975.

Hegel, Georg Wilhelm Friedrich. *Phenomenology of Spirit.* 1807. Trans. A. V. Miller. Annot. J. N. Findlay. Oxford: Oxford University Press, 1977.

Heidegger, Martin. *Being and Time.* 1927. Trans. John MacQuarrie and Edward Robinson. New York: Harper & Row, 1962.

Heidegger, Martin. *Sein und Zeit.* 1927. Frankfurt am Main: Vittorio Klostermann, 1977.

Hobbes, Thomas. *Leviathan.* 1651. Ed. C. B. MacPherson. London: Penguin Group, 1968.

Kant, Immanuel. *Grounding for the Metaphysics of Morals*. 1785.
Trans. James W. Ellington. Indianapolis, Indiana and Cambridge,
Massachusetts: Hackett Publishing, 1981.

Kant, Immanuel. *Critique of Pure Reason*. 1781. Trans. Werner S.
Pluhar. Indianapolis, Indiana and Cambridge, Massachusetts: Hackett
Publishing, 1996.

Kierkegaard, Søren. *The Concept of Anxiety: A Simple Psychologically
Orienting Deliberation on the Dogmatic Issue of Hereditary Sin*. 1844.
Ed. and trans. Reidar Thomte, with Albert B. Anderson. Princeton,
New Jersey: Princeton University Press, 1980.

Kierkegaard, Søren. *Fear and Trembling. Repetition*. 1843. Ed. and trans.
Howard V. Hong and Edna H. Hong. Princeton, New Jersey: Princeton
University Press, 1983.

Kierkegaard, Søren. *Philosophical Fragments. Johannes Climacus*. 1844.
Ed. and trans. Howard V. Hong and Edna H. Hong. Princeton, New
Jersey: Princeton University Press, 1985.

Kierkegaard, Søren. *Concluding Unscientific Postscript to the
Philosophical Crumbs*. 1846. Ed. and trans. Alastair Hannay.
Cambridge: Cambridge University Press, 2009.

Luther, Martin. *D. Martin Luthers Werke: Kritische Gesammtausgabe*.
Vol. 40.1. Weimar: Hermann Böhlaus Nachfolger, 1911.

Luther, Martin. *Selections from His Writings*. Ed. John Dillenberger.
New York: Doubleday, 1961. *Preface to the Epistle of St. Paul to
the Romans*. 1522. Ed. and trans. Bertram Lee Woolf. *Preface to the
Epistles of St. James and St. Jude*. 1522. Ed. and trans. Bertram Lee
Woolf. *The Freedom of a Christian*. 1520. Trans. W. A. Lambert. Rev.
Harold J. Grimm. *A Commentary on St. Paul's Epistle to the Galatians.
(Selections)*. 1531. Rev. and ed. Philip S. Watson.

Marx, Karl. *Capital: A Critique of Political Economy*. 1867–1883.
New York: International Publishers, 1967.

Melville, Herman. *Moby-Dick; or, The Whale*. 1851. Ed. Hershel Parker
and Harrison Hayford. New York and London: W. W. Norton, 1967.

Milton, John. *Paradise Lost*. 1667. Ed. Scott Elledge. New York and
London: W. W. Norton, 1975.

Minkowski, Hermann. "Space and Time." 1908. *The Principle of
Relativity*. Trans. W. Perrett and G. B. Jeffrey. Annot. A. Sommerfeld.
New York: Dover Publications, 1952.

Robinson, Marilynne. *Gilead*. New York: Farrar, Straus, Giroux, 2004.

Tillich, Paul. *Dynamics of Faith*. New York: Harper, 1957.

Tillich, Paul. *The Courage to Be*. 1952. 3rd edn. New Haven,
Connecticut: Yale University Press, 2014.

INDEX OF SCRIPTURE

INDEX